♪ Come Fly with Me!

FLYING THROUGH THE YEARS

Chad,

    To paraphrase the Beach Boys — East coast girls may be hip — but for e-mail, "I wish they all could be California girls!"

        Your Buddy,

        Bob Lanzotti

FLYING THROUGH THE YEARS

A Trilogy of Short Tours and Collection of Short Stories

by

LTC Bob Lanzotti (Ret.)

DORRANCE PUBLISHING CO., INC.
PITTSBURGH, PENNSYLVANIA 15222

For information or to order additional books, please write:
Dorrance Publishing Co., Inc.
701 Smithfield Street
Pittsburgh, Pennsylvania 15222
U.S.A.
1-800-788-7654
Or visit our web site and on-line catalog at
www.dorrancepublishing.com

For all the superb soldiers I served with.

Contents

Army Acronyms and Expressions

1. AC — Aircraft Commander
2. ACR — Armored Cavalry Regiment
3. ADC — Assistant Division Commander
4. ADF — Low Frequency Radio Navigational Aid
5. AHC — Assault Helicopter Company
6. AO — Area of Operations
7. APC — Armor Personnel Carrier
8. ASHC — Assault Support Helicopter Company
9. ARA — Aerial Rocket Artillery, AH-1G Cobra Gunships
10. ARCOM — Army Commendation Medal (Green Weenie)
11. Arty — Artillery
12. ARVN — Army of the Republic of Vietnam
13. Ash & Trash — Non-combat missions or sorties
14. Autorotation — Simulated forced landing or landing without power
15. Blivet — Large rubber bladder, usually five hundred gallons, used for air-transporting fuel and water
16. BOHICA — Bend Over, Here It Comes Again! Aviator's prayer at Annual Physical
17. Bravo Delta — or "Broke Dick," which means that aircraft is unflyable
18. CE — Crew Chief
19. CP — Command Post
20. CH — as in CH-47, the "C" means Cargo, and the "H" means Helicopter
21. DEROS — Date Established Return (from) Over Seas
22. DMZ — Demilitarized Zone
23. Donut Dolley — Red Cross girls, who helped bolster morale of troops in field. Sometimes called Biscuit Bitches, Donut Holes, and Pastry Pigs—but we loved them!

24. Dustoff — Med-Evac Helicopters
25. E&E — Escape and Evasion
26. FAC — Forward Air Controller
27. Fast Mover — USAF jet aircraft that brings smoke, usually a F4 Phantom
28. FE — Flight Engineer, non-pilot crew member
29. FSB — Fire Support Base
30. FUBAR — Fucked Up Beyond All Recognition
31. Fuck — "The" is the most frequently written and spoken word in the English language, except in Vietnam, circa 1962 - 1975. Then, the F-word won hands down. At least, we won that one.
32. Gunship — Armed helicopter that provides fire support
33. IFR — Instrument Flight Rules (flying in weather)
34. Infusion Program — Balancing DEROS dates of a deployed unit through personnel transfers.
35. KPCOD — Korean Pussy Cut Off Date
36. NFG — New Fucking Guy
37. MACOM — Major Command
38. OH — Like in OH-13, the "O" means observation.
39. PCS — Permanent Change of Stations
40. Pop Smoke — Colored smoke used to determine where landing desired and to likewise confirm security of LZ
41. Revetment — A parking barricade to provide protection for aircraft against enemy mortar and rocket attack
42. Romeo Foxtrot — Rat Fuck, meaning that things are in turmoil!
43. ROK — Republic of Korea (Army)
44. RON — Remain Over Night
45. Round Eye — An American female
46. RPG — Rocket Propelled Grenade, Soviet weapon used in Vietnam
47. R&R — Rest and Recreation
48. RVN — Republic of Vietnam, South Vietnam
49. Sapper — VC demolitions expert, usually attacks the perimeter defense
50. S2 — Intelligence Officer, "S" means special staff
51. S3 — Operations Officer, battalion through group/brigade level; G3-division and higher
52. Short Timer — Usually anyone who is within 30 days of DEROS

53. Slicky Boy — Korean petty thief
54. Snake — AH-1G Cobra Gunship
55. TET — Vietnamese lunar holiday; also associated with NVA/VC Major Offensive of January 1968
56. Tac E — (Tactical Emergency) Resupply is necessary to sustain tactical superiority
57. TOC — Tactical Operations Center
58. TOE — Table of Organization and Equipment
59. UH — Like in UH-1, the "U" means utility
60. VFR — Visual Flight Rules
61. WETSU — We Eat This Shit Up!
62. Wobbly 1 — Chief Warrant Officer, Grade 1

Introduction

A "short tour" in Army lingo translates to mean about one year away from your family, friends, and the American way. I always thought that calling it a short tour was one of the biggest misnomers in the Army's jargon. Granted one year today, at my age, seems to just fly by; but beginning twelve or thirteen months of continuous duty with unfamiliar people in a far off land can be pretty dreadful and seemingly endless, particularly in the early months. Oh, there have been periods in my life since retiring from a twenty-five-year career in the Army that I would welcome a short tour. Still the Army idiom, short tour, might be better defined as a "hardship tour;" or in wartime, "obligatory tour;" or perhaps, "combat tour."

The ironic thing about short tours is that, while generally dreaded, most military veterans reflect primarily on events and personal experiences that occurred during such tours. I don't know, maybe it's the camaraderie, or the 7/24/365 devotion to duty, but get military people together and small talk usually centers on events and experiences during somebody's short tour. I recently read a book about a Vietnam veteran's one-year experience as a helicopter pilot during 1969. As I read this book, I was surprised at how many different personal events began to flash through my mind. I had three short tours, one to Korea in 1962-1963 and two tours in Vietnam, the first during 1967-1968 and the second, 1969-1970. I thought as I read the book, *Hey, I should write a book like this with my own experiences!* Even if it wasn't published, it could be interesting reading for my children. Hence the genesis of my short story book about my short tours in the U.S. Army.

This book is divided into three sections, one for each tour. The events are presented chronologically. My stories are a compilation of personal experiences that are wildly different, some funny, some heroic, and, unfortunately, some tragic. Some of the events seem unbelievable, yet every story that follows is an event that did indeed occur

1

and can be corroborated by my Army buddies who served as my brothers in arms. The exact dates are too often not given, but they are close—within days of when the event actually occurred. In many cases I will not give names to avoid embarrassment. In other stories I cannot recall the names anyway.

All three of my short tours came during the 1960s, a full decade before aviation became a separate branch in the Army. In those days if you were a rated commissioned officer you were considered a specialist, sort of like being a jock at a prestigious and cerebral school of higher learning. I would imagine that readers of this collection of short stories might be limited to Army aviators. Oh, there may be a few non-rated combat arms officers who might want to confirm the answer to what they sometimes asked their rated counterparts. Remember, "I don't begrudge the flight pay, but how do you earn your base pay?" Or perhaps younger guys might be interested in the dichotomy of what Army aviators did in the sixties, or rather what they got by with, and how policies and procedures have changed over time. Whoever the reader, I am sure you will recall, as you read, stories of your own. I would encourage you to write them down. Naturally I am kicking myself now for not keeping a journal of the events. And why in the world I did not take pictures is a mystery to me.

My initial assignment out of flight school as a second lieutenant was to Ft. Lewis, Washington. My first assignment to the aviation unit organic to the 4th Infantry Division was indeed an eye opener—so many aviators and so few aircraft. The 4th's divisional aviation assets included an aviation company with a handful of rotary winged aircraft OH-13s, and fixed wing L-19s, L-20s, U-8s, and a couple of U-21s. A CH-21 Helicopter Company, the 57th Transportation Company, was assigned at Gray Army Airfield and colocated with the 4th Aviation Company. There were also a couple of the brand new turbine powered UH-1A (Iroquois) helicopters assigned to the division. The 4th Aviation Company was over strength, which meant that flying experience for a newly assigned aviator was slow in coming. In addition the 4th Aviation Company was also responsible for assuring that those aviators on ground duty were provided with their annual flight hour requirements.

Clearly I was assigned to a unit where I would not get the flying experience that a new aviator needs to sustain the proficiency achieved at flight school, but my time in the 4th Aviation Company was limited to twelve months. I received orders in the spring of 1962 for the Eighth United States Army that was located in Korea. My assignment was to the 7th Aviation Company of the 7th Infantry Division. I was headed for my first short tour.

My brief duty assignment at Ft. Lewis didn't provide a lot of flight time, but it did provide some quality flying experience. During the fall of 1961, I went to the 4th Aviation Company's annual two-week mountain flying school in the Cascade Mountains, at the foot of Mt. Rainier, and learned the effects of density altitude, updrafts, and down drafts on helicopter flying.

Also during the fall, I joined the 22nd Infantry Battle Group as their combat support helicopter detachment pilot and went to Germany for a one-month maneuver exercise called Operation Long Thrust. The entire Battle Group was airlifted by USAF C-135 jet aircraft and flown nonstop from McChord Air Force Base, Tacoma, Washington, to Frankfort, Germany. Another 4th Aviation Company pilot and I received training from 7th Army pilots and flew their helicopters to get familiar with the maneuver area. While we were both 7th Army certified, it was decided that 7th Army pilots would be used exclusively during the two-week maneuver. To me this decision was initially disappointing but proved to be fortuitous for an unworldly young man like myself.

The other pilot, a captain who had previously served a tour in Germany, wasn't disappointed at all—particularly when told that we were free to travel for the next two weeks. I was not only able to see our Army in Germany but also experienced, for the first time, a European tour. We visited Berlin and Paris during our two weeks of gallivanting around Germany and France. To top it off, since we were not a part of the maneuver, we were authorized a per diem allowance that paid for our unexpected vacation. I learned two of my favorite foreign language words, chateaubriand and cordon bleu, which I used almost every evening. I also learned that the King of Beers definitely did not reside in the United States of America.

There are two incidents that happened at Ft. Lewis after I received my orders for Korea that are worth relating. I believe they set the stage for some of the strange and funny experiences that seemed to come my way during my flying career. The first was a forced landing in an OH-13 caused by an engine failure, the first and last time I would ever experience an engine failure during my some 3000 hours of helicopter flying. For those of you who don't know what a OH-13 is, it's the type of helicopter that was used to med evac wounded during the Korean War, the helicopter you saw in all those M*A*S*H television episodes.

Forced Landing

My mission on one beautiful early fall morning was to fly from Gray Army Airfield, Ft. Lewis, to Whidbey Island Air Naval Station to pick up a colonel and fly him to two NIKE missile sites in the Seattle area. My flight path from Ft. Lewis had me flying northbound, hugging the shoreline of the Puget Sound. It was common knowledge among my Army aviator peers that you might occasionally see a bikini clad female catching some rays while flying over the beautiful homes built along the cliffs that rose above Redondo Beach between Tacoma and Seattle. One pilot had even reported seeing a completely nude sun bather who did not seem to mind being ogled from above. My flight altitude was low enough to avail an eyeful if I should get so lucky.

I was navigating at nap-of-the-earth altitude, on eye-level with the roof tops of the homes on my right and about five hundred feet above the beach to my left. My airspeed was about eighty knots when the engine lost power. My reaction to this emergency was surprisingly automatic. I immediately dropped the collective pitch to maintain rotor r.p.m. and looked for a place to land. The only place to land was obvious, the beach to my left was rock free and smooth. The autorotations practiced in flight school and the few I had performed during my 4th Division OH-13 transition served me well. My glide angle to my selected landing spot appeared perfect. My rotor r.p.m. was within limits and my airspeed was seemingly good. As I approached the beach I began to flare the helicopter to reduce forward airspeed, then applied pitch just a few feet above the beach to decelerate airspeed, then used the rest to cushion the landing of the skids on the sand.

I had successfully landed a helicopter that had had an engine failure without damaging it in any way. I had saved one and felt so satisfied with myself. The sobering thought that I had flown directly over a two-mile stretch of the Bay of Tacoma just minutes before passed through my mind. It was a cheap lesson that I would never forget. Had the engine failed then, I would have had to ditch the helicopter into the bay. The glide ratio of an OH-13 is surprising good, but at the altitude that I passed over the bay, there was lots of opportunity for me and my helicopter to get mighty wet.

After the main rotor came to a halt, I climbed out of the helicopter and was greeted by a few people. They were undoubtedly interested in why my helicopter had descended to the beach so quietly. I proudly explained that I had just successfully performed a forced landing and that I needed to find a telephone to contact my base operations at Ft. Lewis. That's when I was informed that the tide was coming in and, in less than an hour, it would submerge much of the helicopter's engine in salt water if we left it in its present location. I asked, "What can we do?" Someone suggested the obvious, see if you can hover it toward the dike next to the road. I reminded myself that it was an engine failure, but it was worth a try. I tried cranking up the engine but the difficulty of the restart and the sound of the engine convinced me that it wasn't up to the task.

By that time one resourceful guy offered what seemed like a good solution. He said that if we could tie a rope to the front skids, perhaps we could drag it toward the dike to higher ground. That should at least keep the engine from getting contaminated with salt water. While I called my flight operations, one good samaritan somehow and somewhere found a strong enough and long enough rope to tie to our front skids. Fortunately the sand was not loose, and we (four strong young men including myself) managed with some strain to pull it about one hundred yards toward the dike, which abutted to the waterfront road. We positioned the helicopter perpendicular to the dike and moved it as close to it as possible to escape the rising tide. My rotors just cleared the piling supporting the dike.

My second call to operations revealed that help was on the way. The 57th Transportation Company had launched a CH-21, a banana-shaped, tandem rotor transport helicopter, carrying a maintenance crew. I was told that the maintenance people would remove the OH-13's main rotor and prepare it for a sling-loaded air-recovery. A few minutes later the CH-21 arrived and dropped off the maintenance people, who quickly removed the rotor and prepared the OH-13 for its sling loaded airborne ride back to Ft. Lewis.

Orbiting above and overseeing the operation was one of our new UH-1A Iroquois helicopters. I was told it was piloted by our company commander, Major John Brandenburg, who, a couple of decades later, would become a lieutenant general. When he arrived the water was just lapping at the aft part of my helicopter skids. From his observation above, it appeared that I had skillfully shot my forced landing to an extremely narrow beach, had stopped only a couple of feet in front of the dike, and had somehow avoided a rotor strike with piling that retained the dike.

I flew back to Ft. Lewis in the CH-21 and watched as my helicopter was safely deposited in front of our maintenance hangar. When I reported to our operations, the operations officer informed me that the commanding officer wanted to see me ASAP. I reported to his office where I had never before been. My nervousness and apprehension were immediately dispelled by the happy look on his face. His congratulatory outstretched hand came with the accompanying words, "Lieutenant Lanzotti, that was the finest forced landing I have ever seen. Well done lieutenant!" I shook his hand, then raised my sore, rope burned hand to a smart salute and responded, "Thank you, sir," and said no more.

Racing Against The Tide

DISABLED ARMY H-13 helicopter is lifted from Puget Sound at Redondo Beach by a larger H-21 helicopter from Fort Lewis. Two soldiers stand in water hip deep, holding stabilizing line. The pilot of the H-13 was forced to land in the Sound after craft's engines failed. Rising tide threatened to submerge it.

—(Associated Press Wirephoto.)

This photograph appeared on the front page of the *Seattle Times*. Might have even been more interesting if the readers had only known "The rest of the story!"

A Missed Opportunity

My second pre-tour story came just a month before my tour ended at Ft. Lewis. About the time I received orders for Korea, the 57th Transportation Company (CH-21 Medium Lift Helicopter) stationed at Ft. Lewis was alerted for deployment to Vietnam. At the same time, another CH-21 company from Ft. Meade, Maryland, was likewise ordered to deploy to Vietnam. Both notifications were unexpected, and the near term departure dates necessitated an accelerated logistical and personnel processing effort for both units. At Ft. Lewis men assigned to the 57th had to move families, and this, of course, took people a way from those extensive duties required for readying a unit for overseas deployment. CH-21 rated pilots within the 4th Aviation Company were needed to help ferry the helicopters from Ft. Lewis to Oakland, California, where they would be loaded on a small aircraft carrier for the journey to South Vietnam.

My advance training during my initial entry flight-training course at Ft. Rucker was in the CH-21. I was qualified in the aircraft and eager to again climb in a CH-21 cockpit and fly it. It would be a two day flight southward through Oregon, where we would RON (remain over night), then after delivery at Oakland we would be flown commercially back to Seattle. I was to be a co-pilot for a W3 warrant officer, who I wish not to name for reasons that will be obvious as this story develops.

Our flight southward to our planned overnight stop was uneventful. My CWO pilot in command let me fly the entire flight, from takeoff to landing, and I again felt so very comfortable in the big, ugly, banana-shaped helicopter. Our RON was Bend, Oregon, right in the middle of the state. I remember that an airport employee in a fuel truck pulled up to our aircraft and immediately began hand pumping aviation fuel. We landed six aircraft, and when we went to the airport the next morning, the same guy was topping off the last aircraft. He had been hand refueling all night long.

My story takes place between the time that the refueling started and ended. We stayed downtown and after dinner stopped at our hotel lounge for a nightcap. The female bar tender was one of the most striking women I had ever laid eyes on, and this was before the first drink! I could not keep my eyes off her. After too many drinks, reinforced with liquid courage, I asked her what she was doing after she got off work. Her response startled me. She said bluntly that she could not walk out with me from the bar, but that we could meet at an all-night diner just a couple of blocks from the hotel. Every word that came out of her mouth as she gave me directions to our rendezvous point exuded the passion I had been fantasizing for the past couple of hours.

One thing I decided immediately: I had had too much to drink and needed to rest to ready myself for my meeting with this goddess. She had almost three hours until she closed and I certainly didn't need to stay and continue drinking. I turned to my good friend, shared with him my good fortune, and told him that I needed to stop drinking and go log some sleep before the rendezvous of my life. He said he was going to stay around for an hour or so and would wake me upon his return to his room that was next to mine.

His wake-up call never came. My good friend forgot or haphazardly gave up a lame attempt to wake me. My wake-up came from another fellow 4th Aviation Company pilot who had wisely skipped a nightcap after dinner. Together we took a cab to the airport and began preflighting our respective aircraft. The warrant officer instructor pilot I was flying with had not arrived as yet, so I proceeded to complete the preflight and flight planning for the remainder of our trip.

About ten minutes before our planned takeoff, a taxicab drove up near our aircraft, my aircraft commander got out and headed for his cockpit seat. After adjusting his seat belt and shoulder harness, he asked me if I could take us to our destination. I told him no sweat, I'm just following the leader. He said, "I know, but I had a hell of a night, I mean, a hell of a morning, and I'm going to grab some shuteye."

After we were airborne and before he was able to doze off, I decided I needed to ask him something, because I had a feeling he had experienced something that was meant for me. So I said, "You had a good time, huh?" He responded by telling me he had gone to a little diner not too far from the hotel and had seen that lovely bartender from our hotel lounge. He went on, "I asked her if she was waiting for somebody as she kept looking toward the door. We continued to talk, and I asked her if she wanted company. She did and she also wore me out!" I shared my story and we laughed. Then he began to reveal some intimate details of his adventure that I did not need to hear, but of course, wanted to hear. He was a likable guy, but I couldn't help but not to like him as I watched him snooze as we flew our last leg to Oakland.

It was the last time I ever felt the controls of a CH-21, but it was not the last time that I would see the warrant officer who had subbed for me at Bend, Oregon. I saw him once in each of my two Vietnam tours that would come during the next decade. At each meeting we immediately began recanting the night at Bend, Oregon. His recall was always more spirited than mine.

Tour One:

Korea

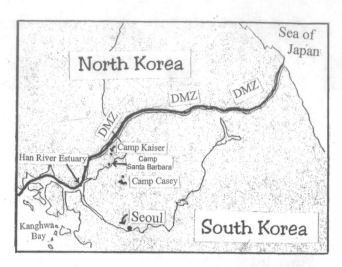

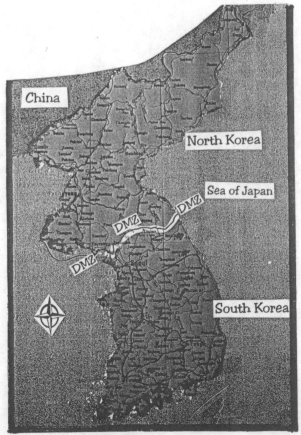

Land of the Morning Calm

My orders to Korea stated that I would depart from Oakland, California, on a troop ship called the *USS Mitchell*. The trip would take twenty-three days with overnight stops in Honolulu and Yokohama. The twenty-three days counted as tour time, so I figured by the time I arrived, about one-thirteenth of my tour would already be completed. This was a new adventure for me. I don't think I had ever been on a boat longer than a fourteen-foot fishing boat. I was one of about twenty Army officers on the ship together with three hundred plus enlisted, all bound for Korea. There were some dependents and several military retirees who were going as far as Hawaii.

The phrase, "Rank has its privileges," became very apparent to me soon after we got underway. If there was such a thing as first class accommodations on a troop ship, I had them. I shared a topside cabin with another officer. The room was large enough to hold two bunks, a desk, and a couple of comfortable reading chairs. It also had a couple of small round windows that could be opened and secured for fresh air. Right next to our room was an exercise room that was well equipped with weights and other exercise apparatus. The Navy had contracted Philippine nationals to clean, cook, and maintain the ship, so not only did I have comfortable quarters, but I also enjoyed room service. Since we had dependents bound for Hawaii, recreational activities were planned nightly after dinner. The food was plentiful and delicious. What a way to travel! I decided early on that if I had my say so, I would definitely request a return trip back to Oakland on the *USS Mitchell*, besides, it would knock another twenty-three days off my thirteen month tour.

The accommodations for the enlisted were the antithesis of what I was experiencing. Their sleeping bays were cramped and hot, and because of seasickness, the odor of vomit was ever present. Each officer was assigned a job for the entire trip, and since I was the designated

Provost Marshal, I spent quite a bit of time in the enlisted limited recreational and living compartments. My duty responsibility was to supervise the nightly duty watch detail that I saw no real reason to have. There was little to watch but the vast ocean. I was also responsible for any discipline problems and administering corporal punishment. I can't recall a single incident and was pleased that confinement of anyone to the brig, a cramped cell near the bow of the ship, was necessary.

One evening when I walked out on the ship's decks to check the guard detail, I was startled by a guard who addressed me not by rank, but by my first and last name. The guard on duty, a PFC, turned out to be a fellow University of Illinois classmate and friend. He had been drafted and would spend about one-half of his service obligation in Korea. We reminisced for a while, and he volunteered how he used to make fun of his fraternity brothers who dressed in their military uniforms to attend advanced ROTC drill. Now, he admitted, the joke was on him, and he wished he would have made a different choice when advanced ROTC enrollment was his option. I was glad I had made the right choice.

The night in Honolulu was all too brief, and I knew I would return someday for a longer stay. The evening in Yokohama was not enjoyable. I didn't care for the dinner I ordered. I was uncomfortable with the strange language, customs, and smells around me. I was thankful to board the ship for our final leg to Korea. But if Japan was a cultural shock, my introduction to my new home for the next year was super seismic beyond my comprehension.

The *USS Mitchell* anchored in the shallow harbor of Inchon, and we were ferried from ship to shore by smaller navy cutters. Our in-processing was accomplished at Inchon and new Army replacements boarded buses for their respective assignments throughout Korea. My destination, the 7th Division, took our bus through Seoul, then north for another forty miles. Fortunately, one of the few paved roads in Korea existed in our direct route to the 7th Division headquarters located in Tongduchon. In fact, there was only one paved road north out of Seoul. Our morning drive was scenic and seemed to be right out of the pages of *National Geographic*. Our arrival coincided with the rice planting season and the "Land of the Morning Calm," as Korea was called, was replete with a low hanging fog that hovered over the watery rice fields, permeating the lower atmos-phere with the unmistakable scent of dung. Farmers worked in fields with their hands and their oxen. While I was half-way around the world, I felt as if I was in another world as the bus drove me to my new assignment.

New Guy on the Block

Reporting to a new unit as just another Indian is, at best, an underwhelming experience. Not surprisingly it's just the opposite when a chief joins a new unit. A chief commands instant respect, loyalty, and attention. I was to learn this later in my career when I reported to units as the incoming new commander, but I absolutely dreaded the first month or so after joining a unit as an Indian. It was a period where you needed to stay low, stay quiet, observe, and just do your job to the best of your ability. Fitting in and finding your comfort zone seemed like miles away. Then one day it just miraculously came. It was like that in the first unit I joined, and it seemed as though that experience would repeat itself, however, I may have gained one distinct advantage to help ease the anguish of this awkward period.

It's funny how decisions and choices made long ago seem to guide your destiny. Raising my hand that I was interested in a newly established ROTC flight-training program at the University of Illinois would ultimately mean a service career in Army aviation, and after that, another decision would have even a greater impact on my future in the army. I was commissioned as a USAR second lieutenant upon graduating from the University of Illinois ROTC program. In 1960 the draft was ongoing. Your chances of entering the military and serving a two-year enlistment were about fifty-fifty. ROTC commissioned officers in that era were either getting six months or two years when called to active duty. It just seemed to me that serving as an officer would beat serving as enlisted, so I signed up for advanced ROTC. It was an easy grade and provided a little extra monthly income that came in handy if you were interested in coeds, and I was. A career in the military didn't even enter my mind during my college years.

I entered the Army and attended the Armor Basic course at Ft. Knox during the summer of 1960. I completed basic officer training in August, and since my Initial Entry Rotary Wing Helicopter training at

Ft. Wolters, Texas was not scheduled until December, I was given an interim assignment at the School Brigade. My company commander, Captain John Potter, learned that I had been on the Fighting Illini football squad for four years at the University of Illinois, and he informed me that I would be the 1960 School Brigade football coach. I could not have had a better coaching opportunity as the majority of my players, most of them officers, had played college ball. Because of our talent and experience, we won often and usually by a wide margin. I became popular with both my company commander and the brigade commander.

Captain Potter, who had won a battlefield commission in the Korean War, suggested that I consider making the Army a career and apply for a Regular Army commission. I liked him and respected him very much. My decision to take his advice was the second major decision that impacted my future in the Army. With several other applicants, I went before a board of officers at Ft. Knox, and was the only one selected. I soon learned that trading in my USAR serial number, 05510733, for my new RA serial number, 094101, did make a difference. Only military academy graduates and ROTC Distinguished Military Graduates were commissioned as Regular Army Officers. Officers possessing a six digit serial number were, I believe, more favorably scrutinized when jobs and responsibilities were handed out.

After my in-country OH-13 checkout at Camp Casey at Tongduchon, home of the 7th Aviation Company, I was selected to assume command of the combat support flight detachment that supported the 1st of 17th Infantry, an organic battle group of the 7th Infantry Division that was located about twenty miles north of the division headquarters. The 17th Infantry Buffaloes shared their compound with another division battle group, the 3rd Infantry. The compound, named Camp Kaiser, was less than two miles from the Demilitarized Zone, the border separating South and North Korea. It was also located near the small Korean village, Unchon-ni. My detachment consisted of one OH-13 helicopter and a crew chief. I shared a small hanger with the other OH-13 detachment supporting the 3rd Infantry. Both detachments were provided room and board by our respective supported units.

The Old Pilot

The Old Pilot that appears on the front cover of this book is not a new picture. I believe the original was an actual photograph that included a witty caption like, "Sleep Well, Your Air National Guard is Ready," or something close to that. It was a fairly popular picture that I had seen in other military clubs of all services, particularly in those frequented by pilots. Our 7th Aviation Company Officer's Club at Camp Casey had a framed picture of the Old Pilot on its wall, together with another framed photograph of the ugliest woman imaginable. It had to be a composite picture, for god could not be that cruel. She was called Modine Gunch. Whoever came up with expression, "coyote ugly," must have seen the photograph of Modine Gunch. Modine's place in the club was beside the Old Pilot.

One of my fellow officers showed me a painting of the Old Pilot, done by an artist from Tongduchon, the Korean town adjacent to Camp Casey. It was an exact replica, in color, and beautifully done. I had not yet visited Tongduchon, but getting a duplicate of the Old Pilot seemed like a good reason to do so. My friend agreed to go with me and help me find the artist. With a 35mm photo of the Old Pilot and some Korean currency in hand, off we went to Tongduchon.

The place of business was hardly a studio. There was no art displayed, but there were brushes, paints, frames, and an easel. He spoke no English, but he knew what I wanted. He kept shaking his head negatively. It finally became apparent that he could not do the work because he had no parchment or canvass on which to paint the picture. We were about to leave when he pulled my light colored rayon shirt, indicating that it could be spread over the picture frame he had in his other hand. I removed my shirt, and he went to work. He completed the picture in less than a half-hour and did a magnificent job.

The Old Pilot painting has been in my possession for forty years now. The picture has always resided above a commode in the bathroom, most likely to accommodate guests. Counting my current residence, I have placed it above eighteen different commodes since I carried it shirtless through Camp Casey's main gate in 1962. I only wish I had packed two light colored rayon shirts for my short tour, because I have always regretted not having that Korean artist paint Modine Gunch for me.

The picture of me on the back cover was taken in Vietnam in 1970 when I was thirty-three years old. To date nobody using my bathroom has asked if the picture above the commode is of me; still, I am beginning to realize that the resemblance gap is closing. Tommy Trinder once said, "There are three ages of man: young, middle age, and don't he look good."

Hail to the Chief

Okay, granted...commanding an aviation combat support flight detachment ain't much, but I was reporting to a new unit as a chief, not an Indian. My arrival was much different from my arrival at my first two duty assignments. I was welcomed and accepted immediately as a fellow Buffalo. Perhaps my stature was elevated by the close relationship that many expected would most assuredly occur between the battle group commander and myself. After all I would soon become his flying aide-de-camp. We would be spending a lot of time together. Then again maybe it was the fact that Colonel Baird had on his staff several aviators who took me under their wings, so to speak. Whatever it was, this was clearly one outstanding unit, and I felt part of its pride as I met the staff and toured the line units.

I learned the word *Camaraderie* from the officers and men of the 17th Infantry. I had learned from sports how to recognize good teamwork as well as how important it was to success. Camaraderie, the military word for teamwork and brotherhood, had the same effect on military performance. The 17th Infantry reeked of camaraderie. It also had the well-established reputation of being the best battle group in the division. The Buffaloes had achieved the highest division scores in its annual Army Training Test (ATT), its Command Material Maintenance Inspection (CMMI), and its Annual General Inspection (AGI). I don't know if it was the first or second day after joining the Buffaloes that I had become convinced that this unit was as good as its reputation.

The Raid

The 31st Infantry, another battle group of the 7th Infantry Division, was collocated with the division headquarters at Camp Casey, some twenty miles to our south. During the Sino-Japanese War, the 31st was presented the Shanghai Bowl, a large, ornate, silver punch bowl, for protecting the lives and property of American citizens in the Yangze area of China. In 1941 the bowl was buried on Corregidor Island before it could fall into the hands of the invading Japanese Army. It was recovered in 1945 after the war and has remained the prized trophy of the 31st ever since.

We learned about the history of the Shanghai bowl from our Buffalo executive officer, a burly lieutenant colonel who had earlier in his career won the Army heavyweight boxing championship. He had served with the 31st previously and told us that the bowl was always displayed in the garrison headquarters. He then announced that the Buffaloes needed to go capture that bowl and bring it back to the Buffalo's Officer Club. When safely in the confines of the Buffalo Club, we would fill it with OB (Korean brew) and drink heartily to celebrate our victory. The XO was idolized by everyone in the battle group, and naturally all thought his plan was brilliant. The plan included me. I was given the job of driving the get-away helicopter. My mission was to land at the division helipad, keep the rotors turning, and wait for the bowl to be delivered. Then I was to high tail it back to Camp Kaiser and carry the bowl to the Buffalo Club.

There was a little problem that gave me reason to dread being a player in this raid. The division aviation officer, a lieutenant colonel and an academy graduate, was a no-nonsense hardass and reputed to be death on those who abused or misused his aircraft. I had just learned that he had recently grounded one of our company helicopter pilots for a month for just nicking a tail rotor blade. I shuddered to think what his reaction would be if he found out how I was employing one of his aircraft to support the infantry in this manner.

The raid went according to plan—sort of. A sergeant in the orderly room where the Shanghai Bowl was encased sensed that the colonel and his entourage were up to no good upon their entry. The sergeant reached for the phone, only to have it ripped from his hand and the line cut by one of the Buffalo perpetrators. The glass encasement was shattered, the bowl secured and hastened to my waiting helicopter. I flew to Camp Kaiser, landed at the Buffalo helipad, and carried the heavy bowl to the Buffalo Club. We waited for the raiding party to arrive by jeep. Two hours after the heist, we were drinking OB beer out of the bowl as planned.

I did not hear a thing from my immediate supervisor, my company commander, or the division aviation officer. Either nobody heard about it, or the prank was overlooked because of the 17th Infantry's notoriety of being a unit that played hard, but performed its mission above and beyond the other division battle groups. Whatever the reason, it appeared that I was home free on this one. What I did not realize was that this incident was typical of what I would be involved with as long as I was associated with the Buffaloes.

My New Country Club

The Buffalo Club consisted of two large rooms. One section served as the officer's mess and the other, the Buffalo Lounge. A walled partition separated the dining room from the lounge. The surface of the wall facing the lounge was decorated with thousands of beer cans affixed to the wall in some manner. The lounge contained a game room with several pool, ping pong, and card tables. Pictures of Buffaloes decorated the walls. Above the bar was a large framed photograph of Korean fire truck that had been stolen from Seoul and driven sixty miles north to Camp Kaiser by an earlier assigned chaplain. The chaplain was seated in the driver's seat in the photograph. Below the photograph was a brass placard with the engraved words, "Stolen by Father (name omitted)!"

The bar hostess was an attractive Korean female. Another young and equally attractive female was employed by the club as a barber. For as little as two dollars you could sit in her chair for about an hour and get the works: shave, shampoo, haircut, manicure, mud pack, and facial message. Koreans had a knack for barbering. I was to learn during subsequent short tours in Vietnam that the Korean's penchant for barbering mastery had apparently not penetrated westward to Vietnam. I never had a bad haircut in Korea and I never had a good one in Vietnam.

Sustaining Camaraderie

The 17th spent a lot of time in the field, but when we were in garrison, the Buffalo Club abounded with activity and energy. Perhaps it was just good chemistry between the assigned officers or maybe it was the leadership provided by the higher ranking officers, but whatever it was, this was truly a unit that exemplified the kind of *esprit de corps* that would be the envy of any commander. All conducted their professional business in the field in a no-nonsense manner of efficiency and effectiveness, but their conduct in the club was sometimes, well maybe the word "outrageous" best describes it.

For example, shortly after joining the Buffaloes, I witnessed several of my new Infantry comrades running down a fellow officer who was about to depart on leave to meet his wife in Hawaii. The capturing officers wrestled this poor chap to the floor, removed his pants and shorts, and painted his private appendage with a liquid called ginseng violet. I do not know what ginseng violet is used for, but I am certain that its purpose was never intended to be this insidious. Ginseng violet's contact with skin leaves a purplish stain that cannot be washed off or rubbed off by friction. Its stain is not permanent but, like old soldiers, just fades away with time—a lot time. You could be assured that it would remain there throughout the duration of a one or two week rendezvous with the partner that you were traveling thousands of miles to get intimate with once again.

Can you imagine the conversation preceding the intimacies of a couple who had been separated for several months? Or her first glimpse of his newly acquired purplish manhood? I would witness this prank a couple of times during my stay with the Buffaloes. I knew that if I decided to take a leave, it would have to be processed by my parent unit, so I felt relatively safe.

A Jim Beam Birthday

One of the company commanders was an academy graduate by the name of Joe Stringham. Joe was destined to become a general officer later in his career. I had befriended Joe shortly after my arrival and used to accompany him as he walked the dirt streets of Unchon-ni to check on his enlisted men who were on pass. Joe, I thought, was the epitome of an Infantry company commander. Everyone liked, admired, and respected him.

His platoon leaders and several of his NCOs decided to throw a party to celebrate his birthday. Somebody, probably his mother, had sent him a bushel of apples as a birthday present. We celebrated his promotion by drinking Jim Beam straight from the bottle and chasing the whiskey with apples. When the party broke up, there were more empty Jim Beam bottles than people who had attended the party. It was by far the worst hangover I have ever experienced. I could not get out of bed the next day and the sickness lingered on for several days. I probably had alcohol poisoning but was too dumb to realize it and too embarrassed to get help. To this day I wouldn't drink Jim Beam if it was given to me and for years I was sure I could detect its presence in party punches.

Party Off, Party On

As a result of the Cuban Missile Crisis during October of 1962, every overseas U.S. military unit was placed on full alert. We were confined to our installations for about three weeks and could not even maneuver in adjacent training areas. Everyone was going stir crazy with the confinement and inactivity. Many of the enlisted who had found love in all the wrong places were getting restless too. There were several reported incidents of love liaisons that had somehow been consummated through the barbed wire fencing that confined our compound.

Officers of the 17th Infantry Buffalo Club were likewise perturbed because a planned early November party had to be scrubbed. The significance of this party was that several American women, known as round eyes, had been invited and had accepted the invitation. The women were nurses, teachers, and Special Services employees. Some of our favorite Red Cross girls who we had met in the field had also been extended an invitation and were likewise coming.

Now a funny thing happened the week the alert was lifted. We found out that I Corps Artillery, stationed at Santa Barbara, about ten miles to our south, was having their annual Artillery Ball that coming weekend. It was a formal affair (dress mess blues) that seemed well suited for the combat arms branch that bragged of lending dignity to the battlefield. We also learned that all the round eyes we had invited to our canceled party would be there. Our XO, who masterminded the Shanghai Bowl raid, wasted no time in laying out a new fail-safe stratagem that would turn on the Buffalo party that had been turned off because of the alert.

He announced that we would kidnap the girls and carry them from Santa Barbara to Camp Kaiser and show them what serious partying was all about. His plan, like most good plans, was simple and included the element of surprise. I was relieved to learn that his plan this time did not include the use of the helicopter. Transporting the girls would be accomplished by trucks. As stated earlier, the colonel was well known and well liked by everyone. He was Mr. Stud and would have undoubtedly won a popularity contest with John Wayne among the troops. There was a 7th Division Military Police detachment at Camp Kaiser, and the plan would have to have their cooperation—not their active participation, but just the use of some of their MP paraphernalia for a few hours.

The 17th Infantry raiding party, decked out in MP gear departed Camp Kaiser in a convoy of one jeep and two trucks. Upon arrival at the I Corps Officers Open Mess, the XO entered the ballroom, walked straight across the dance floor to the band section, and motioned the band to stop playing their music. Dressed in his MP helmet, replete with an attached lieutenant colonel's leaf as well as all the other gear that made him look legitimate, the XO grabbed the microphone, and announced: "Ladies and gentlemen, I apologize for the intrusion, but our Navy has just sunk its first ship off of Cuban shores, and we have been dispatched to evacuate all noncombatants."

The artillerymen just stared dumbfounded at this high ranking MP, but several higher ranking officers began scurrying to find some way to communicate with their unit operations. Time was of the essence, particularly since girls, being girls, couldn't leave without their overnight belongings. The 17th Infantry MPs hastened the departure as quickly as possible and the convoy departed without being stopped. The getaway was successful, and the ensuing party at the Buffalo Club was just as our leader had predicted; we did indeed show those girls how to party. We would later decorate our club walls with a lot of great photographs of that memorable night.

I don't know if there were any repercussions over this bizarre event. If anybody got into trouble, I sure didn't hear about it. I was beginning to think that this battle group was like the Untouchables.

Instructor Pilot Training

After being with the Buffaloes for about four months, I was notified by my parent unit that I had been selected to become the 7th Aviation Company's instructor pilot for both the H-13 and H-23 aircrafts. My training would be provided by the 55th Aviation Company, a unit located in Seoul near Eighth Army headquarters. Major Ken Calcatera was my instructor pilot, and we hit it off well. After completing my training, I returned to the 17th Infantry to resume my combat support flying role. I mention this training and experience because it would later lead to my reassignment to the 55th Aviation Company to become the Eighth Army OH-13 and OH-23 standardization instructor pilot.

One Last Hurrah with the Buffaloes

If the XO had a partner in crime, it would be the S-3. You would think you were working with Batman and Robin with those two. I was particularly close to the S-3. He and I shared the passion of bird hunting. Since there were pheasants in Korea, he carried his shotgun to the field with him. Several times I radioed him from the helicopter after spotting pheasants while flying, picked him up, and returned to some good shooting. We enjoyed some good pheasant dinners, too, both in the field and back at the Buffalo Club.

One day he informed me that we were going to make a Sunday morning flight to Taegu, about 175 miles to our south, to coordinate a near future joint operation involving the USAF, the 1st Cavalry Division, and a unit from the ROK Army. Now the S-3 had a proclivity for some serious beer drinking. He had downed a couple of brewskis before our Sunday morning departure and indulged during our flight down to Taegu as well. Frankly, I was afraid for him because he had to make a presentation before some pretty high ranking folks.

His performance was phenomenal, the best of the show. I guess he decided to celebrate his feat, because he continued his airborne guzzling on our return flight. As we approached Santa Barbara, the home of I Corps Artillery and no friend of the Buffaloes, my passenger said, "Let's land at the I Corps helipad; I need to go into the club." He was out of beer, and I was running out of patience. I thought to myself, *can't this guy wait until he gets home for another beer?* After all, we were only about ten minutes from Camp Kaiser! The I Corps officer's club was within a hundred or so yards from the helipad. I was told to keep the rotors turning because he wouldn't be long. Within five minutes after entering the club, he came bounding out the front door with an armful of what appeared to be plaques. They were plaques—all the artillery battery crests of all U.S. units assigned in Korea. He jumped in the helicopter with people running toward us, and I lifted to a hover, stopping them short.

The crests were returned within a couple of days. Apparently, I Corps had no problem determining who the culprits were, but again, I never heard a thing about this incident. It was about this time that I learned that my time with the Buffaloes was coming to an end. My company commander informed me that the 55th Aviation Company had requested that I be reassigned to 8th Army to become the OH-13 and OH-23 standardization instructor pilot for all aviation units assigned in Korea.

I will never forget my time with the Buffaloes. Here was a unit that clearly should have had some admonishments, yet they kept getting accolades for performance when it really counted and that seemed to excuse their outlandish antics at other times. I don't believe I was ever in a more spirited unit, and it was a great experience to have early in my career. I was proud to have been a Buffalo and still cherish the Buffalo brass memento I was given when I departed for my new assignment.

Country Mouse, City Mouse

Roughly half of my six months with the 17th Infantry was spent in the field. I didn't mind it in the fall but despised it during the winter months. My new assignment to the 55th Aviation Company would mean that my days in the field would be coming to an end. Life with the 55th Aviation Company would be quite a contrast to what I had experienced with the 17th. The living conditions would be much improved. One hundred percent of the time in a BOQ room sure beats spending 50 percent of my nights in a CP tent. Also the memory of seeing a swimming pool next to the 55th Aviation Company Officer's Club during my instructor pilot training had not escaped me.

My new home, the 55th Aviation Company, was located at K16, a sandbar island in the middle of the Han River that ran through the southern outskirts of Seoul. Our neighboring suburbs of Seoul were Yongsong and Yongdongpo. The Eighth Army headquarters was located across the river and about five miles to our northeast. The compound encompassing Eighth Army Headquarters was known as Seoul Army Command (SAC). Its Officers Club and facilities would rival anything in the states. I thought it pretty clever that the biggest PX in all of Korea was located on SAC's Fifth Avenue. I was truly in a different environment. I had gone from the sticks to the suburbs, and all because I could fly the hell out of an OH-13.

The Arrival

The primary mission of the 55th Aviation Company was to provide aviation support for the Eighth Army commanding general and his staff. In addition 55th aviators provided standardization instructor pilot training in all fixed and rotary wing aircraft for all aviation units assigned within the Eighth Army Command. Upon my arrival I met with the company commander. It was Major Calcatera who had qualified me only a month or so earlier as an instructor pilot. He informed me that my primary job was to provide standardized OH-13 and OH-23 flying instruction to qualify pilots to perform instructor pilot duties at their home units. I would also fly or assist in flying high-ranking Eighth Army officers, often generals, all over the peninsula of South Korea.

In preparation for this task, I was to immediately begin transition training to be qualified to fly the relatively new turbine powered UH-1A Iroquois helicopter, dubbed the "Huey." Needless to say, I was pumped. After this meeting I was escorted by the officer I would be rooming with and toured the company area to meet my fellow officers and the key noncommissioned officers. There were about twenty-five assigned aviators in the company.

The Initiation

During the tour of the company area, I was told that I could expect to be initiated into the club that evening. Before being informed of this, I had been asked if I was a teetotaler. I assured my new roommate that I was not against partaking, but I sensed a hint of foreboding in the question and wondered what in the world was in store for me that evening. I had experienced a fraternity hell week in college and thought, *This couldn't be any worse!* Bad assumption. It was worse.

That evening I was to told that I would gargle a mouthful of rum for sixty seconds along with the guy who was last initiated as a club member. This didn't sound difficult, but I was soon to learn that the rum to be gargled, called "Lemon Heart," was a 180 proof British rum that was about as flammable as JP4. At the time of reckoning, I was told that I should spew my rum mouthwash on the bar following the one minute gargle. I would discover that the length of time condensed in one minute can seemingly vary from seconds to hours. I would also live to see my rum mouthwash emit a flame that would rival any aviation fuel. Then I alone (the last initiate was excused from this ordeal since he had done it as a part of his ceremony) would have a shot of Lemon Heart rum with every pilot in the unit. This meant that a new 55th Aviation Company initiate would, on the average, have about twenty or so jiggers of Lemon Heart before he finished drinking with all of his new aviator cohorts. Now the trick is: you can down Lemon Heart, but you should not *keep* it down. For that reason, there should be several visits to the restroom to undrink the stuff.

When the drinking ordeal was finished, the new initiate was driven to the infamous Green Door, a Korean whorehouse in Yongdongpo, a southern suburb of Seoul. I never could figure out why this was a part of the initiation, because even if someone had been so inclined, who in the world could perform after consuming Lemon Heart? Despite the upchucking, some of that stuff stayed in your system, and a little went a long way toward putting you over the top. I couldn't remember the trip to Green Door or the time I spent there. I do know that if the initiation had to be consummated in that manner, then I did not make the team.

The Lemon Heart initiation ceremony didn't last long after my initiation. Perhaps, five to ten initiates after me, one poor fellow who failed to throw up what he had thrown down, eventually ended up going down—like, unconscious down. Several U8 qualified pilots carried him to the flight line and tried reviving him using oxygen on board one of our U8 aircraft. About that time our flight surgeon, who had been summoned, arrived on the scene and took over.

Dr. Pete Rank, the only flight surgeon who I can still recall by name, made quite an impression on all of us that evening. He assembled all the officers in the club. There was absolute silence for a couple of minutes as he glared at all of us. When he did begin speaking it was evident that he was livid with anger and disgust. He told us that Lemon Heart was henceforth banned from our club, as were all the silly initiations that involved binge drinking. He told us that we had come very close to killing one of our fellow officers, and that had a sobering impact on all of us. Nobody missed Lemon Heart rum, and 55th Aviation Company initiations were history.

Short-Timers Table

The 55th had two mess halls, one for its officers and one for the enlisted. The officer mess hall's dining room included a center table for six that was quite different from the other tables that surrounded it. The center table was elevated on a platform about eight inches above the floor level. It was always draped with a clean white tablecloth and decorated with china, silver, crystal, and even a candelabra. This table was reserved exclusively for the six shortest officers in the unit, not in terms of stature, but for those who had the fewest number of days left in their tour. There was an order of seniority at the table. The table was headed by the short-timer who was next to take a big freedom bird eastbound to the western hemisphere. His official title was the Grand Dictator, but he was called the Grand Dick. To his right sat the Enforcer, who was just one heart beat away from the Grand Dick. At the far end of the table, opposite the Grand Dick, sat the longest short-timer at the table, the Pledge. Advancement in seniority could come only through rotation of its members to a new assignment or a return to the States.

Privileges came with being seated at the short-timers table. First you could drink wine with all your dinner meals. Second you were always served first, no matter what meal it was. And third you would always be given preference for seconds if there was short supply of a particularly favorite item on the menu. The Korean waiter assigned to the table made sure the rules were strictly followed.

There were only two rules for the short-timers seated at the table. First you could not acknowledge the masses or the long-timers seated below you. This meant that you could not talk to them or even glance in their direction. Second you could never mention the dirty, repugnant word "long" during your conversation with fellow short-timers seated at the table. Infringement of either rule would mean that you would have to purchase a bottle of wine for the table. That is the how wine was replenished. It is mighty difficult to omit the word "long" in a long conversation, and the masses were constantly trying to get your attention or response in some manner. There was always plenty of wine to drink. Our selection, however, was limited to two choices, Liebfraumilch or Chateauneuf-Du-Pape. I remember the names because I drank many a bottle.

When I reported to the 55th Aviation Company, I had about seven months remaining on my thirteen-month short tour. Then, a month after my arrival, I was told that I had suddenly become the sixth shortest officer in the unit and would be moving from the masses to the short-timers table. It must have been close to the longest time anyone had ever sat at the short-timers table.

Whoever originated the short-timers table was a genius, for nobody could argue against its merits as a morale builder. To everyone who served in the 55th, getting to the short-timers table was considered a major milestone. I have never seen or heard of another unit that had anything resembling a short-timers table. My two subsequent short tours would have consolidated mess halls where the folly of the short-timers would be inappropriate.

Humbling Helicopter Experience

I don't believe I have ever enjoyed a job in the military more than the one I had as a standardization instructor pilot in the 55th Aviation Company. I suppose a lot of it had to do with the fact that flying was relatively new and I was enjoying it so much. Admittedly, I was also probably a little impressed with myself. I had been rated for only about eighteen months, and here I was performing the duties of a MACOM standardization instructor pilot. I was marveling that someone had actually recognized that I was good at something, and that is why I was where I was and doing what I did. I loved emulating the IPs that had impressed me in flight school as well as those that had given me training since flight school.

I was the Eighth Army standardization IP for both the OH-23 Hiller and the OH-13 Bell, but most Eighth Army units had OH-13 helicopters, and therefore, most of the training I conducted was in the OH-13. If God intended for me to do anything well, I am sure he smiled when I strapped myself to a OH-13. I could flat fly that helicopter. I was particularly good at shooting autorotations to a designated spot. The OH-13 had a remarkable glide ratio and was super maneuverable without power. Put me at any altitude and within glide ratio of any marking on the ground and I could put either skid within an inch of that spot. Performing autorotations was a part of the IP training syllabus that I enjoyed the most. I made it a practice of building a student's confidence and skill throughout the week, then challenging him on the last day of training by shooting autorotations to a designated spot. I never lost.

I got a real dose of reality just about the time that I had become thoroughly convinced that I was the Army's best OH-13 pilot. Reality came one very cold February morning in 1963. I had demonstrated to a student how to perform a low level autorotation. I used a sandbar near Yongson Helipad, the helipad servicing Eight Army headquarters. I demonstrated first, then let the student practice one or two himself before we returned to K16. During our afternoon training we were flying low level over the same area, and I reduced the throttle to simulate an engine failure. The student correctly lowered the collective pitch to maintain rotor RPM, then flared the helicopter to dissipate airspeed. His touchdown was looking good...skids level...a bit fast...but no faster than our touchdowns earlier in the day. The problem was that the sand had been fused a little in the morning because of the freezing temperature but had loosened with the warming temperatures in the afternoon. After touching down, the right skid began to dig into the sand, causing the nose of the aircraft to tilt downward and the tail rotor to rise. Both of us simultaneously pulled back on the cyclic to correct the attitude of the aircraft.

There are dynamic stop cables in the rotor hub assembly to prevent the rotor from flexing down into the tail section, but even stop cables couldn't overcome our yanking of the dual-control cyclics into our laps. The main rotor clipped off the tail section like knife going through butter. The last thing that moved in the helicopter was the instrument console, which detached and fell forward right through the bubble. My student and I released our seat belts and exited the cockpit directly to our front where the console and bubble had been.

Within what seemed like a minute, a MP who had seen the accident from the helipad approached us in his jeep. He asked who the operator of the helicopter was. When I responded that I was the pilot in command, he asked for my operator's license. I assured him that aviators were not required to carry an operator's license and that it wasn't necessary for him to write an accident report.

The helicopter we had just crashed was not the property of the 55th Aviation Company. Students reporting for instructor pilot training brought aircraft from their own units. This aircraft was new OH-13H model from the 1st Cavalry Division. I suddenly started feeling lower than whale dung on the bottom of the deep blue sea. I was responsible for this debacle. I returned to K16 late that evening with a broken helicopter loaded on a flatbed truck. I felt very humiliated and embarrassed when we rolled that truck into our hangar.

Fortunately our unit maintenance officer, Captain Nate Green, had all the parts necessary to put it back into flying order within a couple of days. The very next day I flew with Major Calcatera, who put me through a whole series of autorotations, to include a couple of low level ones. It would be my first and last accident in a helicopter during my army aviation career, thank God.

1st Cavalry Division OH-13, but, flyable and fully intact!

I Don't Think We Are In
Kansas Anymore!

Before leaving on my short tour, my grandmother gave me a small stainless steel Big Ben alarm clock. While stationed at Camp Kaiser, it resided on my night stand beside my bed for about a month before it disappeared. I was told that it had been stolen by a "slicky boy." Korean slicky boys, I was told, were reputedly considered world-class thieves. As the saying goes, "A slicky boy can steal your radio and leave the music behind!" Sometime during the late fall, I wrote my grandmother and informed her how Big Ben had gone AWOL and was now probably ticking away in some Korean's home. She sent me another alarm clock, same brand and model, for a Christmas gift. I kept it secured until my move to my new assignment. Then after my arrival, I displayed the little Big Ben again on my night stand next to my bed. It didn't last there much longer than the first one had stayed in my possession at Camp Kaiser. A city slicky boy had struck this time.

Sometime shortly after my second clock disappeared, I flew a JAG officer to the DMZ to look at some pilferage that was taking place at almost every defensive bunker that bordered our side of the DMZ. It was in the dead of winter and the ground was frozen, yet virtually every four-by-four concrete post used in the construction of the bunkers was somehow extracted from the ground or from the bunker itself, then smashed to smithereens so that the steel reinforcing rod or rods could be taken. It wasn't vandalism; the perpetrators were after the steel which was obviously of some value to them.

I told the JAG officer about my bad luck with trying to keep time with little Big Ben alarm clocks, and he related a fascinating and true story about one Korean slicky boy who ran out of luck and time. The Turks, who fought with us during the Korean War, retained a unit in Korea after the armistice was reached. The Turks were also harassed by thievery until they captured one unfortunate slicky boy. They decapitated this poor soul, then ran a steel rod through the head and displayed it above the main gate of their compound. It was pretty powerful advertising. Slicky Boy activity within the Turk compound ceased. Granted, it didn't do too much toward winning the hearts and minds of the indigenous population, but it sure gave reason to think about good and bad choices for those possessing a proclivity to loot.

On another mission I flew the Eighth Army Deputy Commanding General to a Korean Army unit located about fifty miles northeast of Seoul. The general, who was being escorted through the unit's motor pool by a ROK general officer, stopped at a vehicle and made a comment that he later admitted that he wished he had not made. He commented to the Korean general something to the effect that while the vehicle was probably in tip-top operational condition, it appeared to need some first echelon maintenance (like, it could use a wash job). Minutes later, as the general was leaving the motor pool, we heard a commotion from the vicinity of the vehicle he had criticized and saw a ROK motor sergeant pummeling the driver of the vehicle with what appeared to be a wrench. I suppose a couple of lessons could have been learned from that exchange, both by our general and, perhaps, the ROK motor sergeant; and that is, "One ought to praise in public, and criticize in private."

You Never Get a Second Chance to Make a Good First Impression

When the subject, "My most embarrassing experience" is raised, I generally recall three doozies. One of the three was a bizarre accident involving my helicopter and myself in Korea during the spring of 1963. No, it was not the accident on the sandbar previously mentioned, though that was indeed embarrassing. This accident involved no damage to the helicopter but did severely wound my self-esteem and pride. While I can now laugh about the incident, I can assure you that it was definitely not a laughing matter when it occurred.

During my entire short tour in Korea, I could not have picked a worse time for such a dumb thing to happen. The mission on my day of infamy was to fly the Eighth Army commanding general, General Guy S. Meloy, to the flagship of several U.S. Navy ships anchored off the southern coast of Korea near Pusan. We would land on the flagship's helipad, pick up the admiral of the fleet, and carry them both to bleachers on the beach where they could observe an amphibious exercise involving all U.S. services and some ROK forces. General Meloy had been flown down from Seoul by one of our U21 fixed wing aircraft and was driven to our waiting Huey that was parked on a helipad near the bleachers where he and the admiral were to observe the exercise. The general's assigned pilot and myself, flying as his co-pilot, had flown down to Pusan the previous day to coordinate the mission with our Navy counterparts.

The pick up of the admiral and the flight back to the beachside helipad went smoothly. My job as co-pilot was to stay with the helicopter during the exercise. We moved the helicopter off the helipad but had no means to tie down main rotor blade, and I would have to secure it by hand if another helicopter landed at the helipad. I was instructed to watch the bleacher area and start the helicopter when I saw the general and the admiral get into their ground transportation to return to our helicopter.

Just about five minutes before the general and admiral got up to depart for the helicopter, I observed a CH-37 Sikorsky helicopter making its final approach to the helipad where our helicopter was parked. The CH-37 was the largest helicopter in the Army inventory in 1963. It could generate hurricane force winds below its main rotor blades as it neared the ground for landing. Our helicopter would not obstruct the CH-37's landing to the helipad, but its proximity to where the CH-37 would touch down gave me concern about blowing debris and sand. I had to clamber up the side of the Huey's fuselage to pull the main rotor down so I could grab it with both hands over my head near the tail rotor assembly.

As the CH-37 descended to the helipad, I prepared myself for the oncoming rotor wash by pulling my fatigue hat down on my head as far as it would go without covering my eyes. I then hid behind the tail boom of the Huey to protect myself from the blowing sand that would soon be coming my way. The CH-37 landed, dropped off passengers, then picked up to a hover to begin its ascending departure. As the rotor wash dissipated, I glanced toward the bleachers. To my surprise the general's ground transportation had already departed and was approaching the helipad.

I released the blade and bounded toward the cockpit. I was bound and determined to have the turbines going and the rotors turning when the general's sedan arrived next to our helicopter, but a funny thing happened on my way to the cockpit. You see, my hat was still pulled down low on my head, and I did not see the fixed stabilizers that protrude horizontally from both sides of the aft fuselage near the tail rotor. I hit the left stabilizer at eye level and the force of my collision actually bowled me backwards in what I was told looked like kind of a spastic back flip. I wasn't unconscious when the general arrived over my crumpled body, but I was certainly dazed, yet lucid enough to hear General Meloy ask, "Are you okay, son?" I don't remember if I responded. To this day I don't know what the right response would be. I mean, here at the general's feet was his pilot, who had just run into his own aircraft. It was hardly a good first impression.

An Involuntary Tour Extension

On the morning of May 17, 1963, two 55th Aviation Company pilots, Captains Ben Stutts and Carelton "Bill" Voltz, looked over their mission sheet and began planning their morning flight. The mission was to check the markers that delineate the Military Demarcation Line (called the DMZ), a two and one-half mile wide buffer zone that extends across the entire peninsula and separates North and South Korea. Fixed wing pilots in the 55th were often tasked to conduct aerial surveillance of the DMZ to assure that markings were intact and had not been moved or removed. Both Stutts and Voltz had previously flown such missions but always in fixed wing aircraft. Today's mission was to check the DMZ markers northwest of Seoul along the Han River Estuary. Since the area to be checked was confined to just a few miles, it was decided that a helicopter would be used.

There is, of course, a vast difference when one observes terrain features at different altitudes. Surveillance of the DMZ with fixed wing aircraft was typically conducted at altitudes just below those levels requiring oxygen. At such altitudes several in-line markers might be observed simultaneously. Since Stutts and Voltz were fixed wing standardization instructor pilots, they infrequently flew rotary wing aircraft. Neither had ever flown a helicopter near the DMZ. Further complicating the mission was the fact that the Han River Estuary had flooded from spring rains, distorting visual references on the 1:50,000 maps carried by all aviators. In some cases, the markers that they were looking for on May 17, 1963, were not visible simply because they were under flood waters.

While trying to locate the DMZ markers, both pilots heard what they thought was unusual engine noise. Thinking that they may be experiencing fuel contamination, a precautionary landing was made. Later they would surmise that the engine noise they thought they heard was probably ground fire, something neither had experienced and certainly did not expect. They landed to make a fuel check. Upon touching down, the helicopter was immediately surrounded by uniformed North Korean soldiers pointing 7.62mm weapons in the direction that immediately erased the language barrier. There was no doubt as to what the people pointing their weapons wanted them to do as well as what would happen if they didn't do it. Captain Stutts, U.S.A., and Captain Voltz, U.S.A., exited the OH-23 Hiller helicopter and became captives.

The aircraft was not shut down when they were dragged away, and the rotors continued to turn until the fuel tank was exhausted. When the rotors did stop, the hourglass imprisonment for Captain Stutts and Captain Voltz had already begun.

The news of the lost helicopter and captured pilots hit Eighth Army like a low blow. For the 55th Aviation Company, it was almost a knock-out punch. People in the 55th were devastated. It was on everyone's mind, and few conversations were started and stopped without its mention. When would they be released? What was Eighth Army and our State Department doing to negotiate a release? How were they being treated? What was their status? Were they prisoners of war? Why couldn't the Red Cross visit them? I would leave Korea about three and one-half months from the date of the capture, and these questions and more were still being asked without answers.

Ben Stutts and Bill Voltz were released on May 17, 1964, 365 days after they were taken prisoner. Following their release Bill Voltz completed his service obligation then became a commercial airline pilot for a major airline. Ben Stutts remained in the Army, but was killed later in a Third Army airplane while flying alone in inclement weather.

While on leave in the Chicago area during the late sixties, I learned that Bill Voltz was flying out of O'Hare Field. I contacted him and invited him to dinner. Bill related his one-year hardship tour north of the DMZ in graphic detail. He said that he and Ben did not see each other during their entire confinement. They were separated after they were pulled out of the helicopter and did not see each other again until the day they were repatriated. There were three distinct periods, all about four months in length. Interrogation was the first order of business and the most unpleasant. Both were tortured. Interestingly the torture never left permanent scars on their bodies. Bill Voltz thought, positively and hopefully, that this might mean that they could be released at any time without physical evidence of mistreatment. The second phase was isolation and the last was indoctrination.

I thought it interesting that the interrogators would never accept anything that would indicate that the American society was more advanced than their country. For example Bill said he was beaten when he told them most American families owned televisions, automobiles, refrigerators, and such conveniences as clothes washers and dryers. He felt as if the time of release was coming during the indoctrination phase as he was finally being treated like a human being, and there was actually a sincere effort on the part of the captors to convince him that their society was superior to his homeland.

Bill emphasized over and over during our visit just how much hatred the North Koreans harbor toward America and Americans. That hatred has surely passed with each generation, since little has changed in the past forty years. That two and a half mile buffer, called the DMZ, still extends 151 miles across the peninsula and divides two completely different societies. South Korea has adopted America's capitalistic system and has become, since the Korean war, a modern industrial nation. North Korea, under communism, has gone through famine and remains as backward as the day Bill Voltz tried to convince his captors that most American families owned automobiles, televisions, refrigerators, washers, and dryers.

The Ode

The absence and plight of Ben and Bill had severely dispirited the 55th. Their release and return seemed to be the only way of restoring the kind of morale that existed right up to the time we learned of their capture. The last three months of my tour were fairly uneventful. I moved my way up through the ranks of the short-timers table and was finally seated in the coveted Grand Dick's chair. Heading the short-timers table was a milestone in itself, but there was another established tradition in the 55th worth noting.

Every departing 55th aviator was given a farewell party the night before he was to PCS. No, a visit to the Green Door was not arranged as the departing officer's KPCOD (Korean Pussy Cut Off Date), if he was so inclined to even need one, had already come and gone. The traditional send-off party did include a ritual that revealed information about a departing officer that he would just as soon not carry with him to share with his wife or with the officers of his new duty station. Among men who live in close quarters, events and antics often occur that are best forgotten.

What better place to mention the unmentionable than at one's going away party, where revealing irreverence is expected and retrospection is harmless? That was exactly the key event of the party that everyone enjoyed. The departing officer was seated on a bar stool with his back to the pool between the company commander and a fellow officer by the name of Willis E. Davis. Captain Davis, who would become my company commander at Ft. Benning just a year later, was a gifted writer and volunteered to write an ode for every departing officer. The odes he dedicated and read aloud were replete with most of the transgressions committed by the departing officer during his days with the 55th. His writings included personal idiosyncrasies and anything and everything that might embarrass the guy who was leaving the next day. It was a roast long before celebrity television roasts became vogue. When Willis completed the reading of the ode, the commanding officer would push the departing officer backwards into the pool.

Nobody could figure out how Willis obtained some of the information that went into those odes, but one thing is for certain; he never strayed from the truth, and personalities were always pegged right on. While he managed to embarrass all, none were ever offended. It was great fun for everyone. Following the going away party, the ode was framed and safely displayed for all to see in the officer's club john. After all, there were confidentialities in many of those odes that could be detrimental to one's marriage and profession.

I wish I had a copy of my ode, and I would love to walk into that restroom again and read each and every one that Willis wrote. I remember that my ode referenced my two embarrassing accidents, the sandbar crash and my Huey head butting fiasco, but I do not remember much beyond that. There were probably a couple of other transgressions mentioned that I best leave alone. Perhaps the john was the perfect place to display the gallery of odes.

Goodbye Korea

My return to the real world was by commercial jet, not by troop ship. I had requested a return cruise, but learned that shuttling soldiers to and from Korea by troop ship had been discontinued shortly after my arrival in Korea. My trip home was almost uneventful, but it did yield one final noteworthy story.

I have always been accident prone. I mentioned one of my three most embarrassing blunders earlier. The other two, not mentioned in this book, also involved accidents, not in cars or airplanes but embarrassing nonetheless. The little accident I had on my return flight from Korea would follow me for the rest of my military career.

Servicemen returning from Korea were allowed to carry in their possession five bottles of alcoholic spirits. I selected an assortment of the most expensive liquors that I could buy. The scotch selection was Johnny Walker Black Label. For those of you familiar with this brand, you will know that the glass bottle is very thin and not particularly well suited for travel, unless well protected with packing material. In 1963, officers departing Korea were given their personnel and medical records to carry to their next duty station. One should never drink and drive, and one should never carry records in the same suitcase with booze. Four out of five bottles survived, but Johnny Walker did not make it, and for the next twenty-two years my personnel and medical file would smell like scotch. The smell of alcohol is not the scent you like yourself to be associated with when visiting the flight surgeon or when your file is being reviewed by a board of senior officers considering you for promotion or for other career enhancing opportunities. And I don't even like scotch!

Tour Two:

Vietnam 1

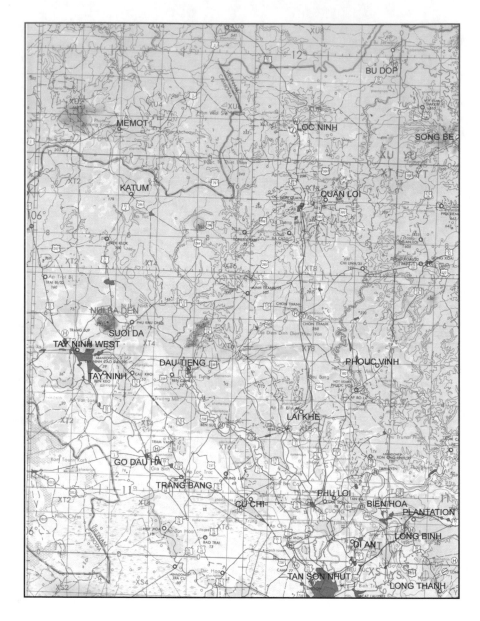

This map was issued to all pilots who flew in the III Corps area of operations. It encompasses all of the Provinces that I flew over during both tours. Virtually every village/city shown in enlarged print is mentioned in the remaining pages; therefore, you might want to bookmark this map for future reference and orientation of events within Tours Two and Three.

(Map furnished by Mike Law, Calendar and Directory Editor of the Vietnam Helicopter Pilots Association.)

Gearing Up for Combat

My duty station after Korea was Ft. Benning, Georgia, where I joined the 2nd Aviation Battalion. I was assigned to Company A, the medium lift CH-34 unit. Alpha Company's primary mission during most of my assignment would be to support the build-up and train-up of the 11th Air Assault Division (Test). The provisional 11th Air Assault Division was conceived at Ft. Benning during February, 1963, with the formation of the Airmobility Concept Board. Within a short year, the 11th Air Assault Division became fully manned and was equipped with the newest rotary wing aircraft, the UH-1 and CH-47. The 11th would train and be tested for the next fifteen months to determine if its airmobility concept was viable and survivable on the modern and unconventional battlefield. On July 1, 1965, the 11th Air Assault Division (Test) was deemed combat ready and was renamed the 1st Air Cavalry Division (Airmobile).

During the early months of 1966, I received orders to report for a nine month Armor Officer Advanced Course at Ft. Knox, Kentucky. The 2nd Infantry Division's imminent replacement of the 1st Cavalry Division's mission in Korea required its stand down at Ft. Benning. That, coupled with my August reporting date to Ft. Knox, gave me an opportunity to attend both the Ranger and Airborne courses at Ft. Benning. Almost thirty years later I would read the names of many of my Ranger classmates in one of the best historic books every written about Vietnam. *We Were Soldiers Once...And Young*, by Lieutenant General Harrold G. Moore (Ret.) and Joseph L. Galloway. One Ranger classmate, Lieutenant Joe Marm, was awarded the Congressional Medal of Honor for valor during the Ia Drang campaign. A great many of my Ranger classmates would immediately deploy with the 1st Air Cavalry Division (Airmobile) after graduation since it was ordered to proceed to Vietnam by President Johnson on July 28, 1965.

I had helped ferry aircraft from Ft. Lewis, Washington, to Oakland, California, to be shipped to Vietnam, then watched the first helicopter unit, a company, deploy to Vietnam during the late spring of 1962. Now I would watch the second unit, this time a whole division, depart for Vietnam. The Vietnam troop build-up was on, and I wondered when I was going to get my chance to go. I wasn't the only one who was getting anxious. Most of my Advanced Course classmates were regular Army officers who, like myself, found WWII tank tactics interesting but were salivating for counter-insurgency instruction. Virtually the entire class would be going to Vietnam upon graduation.

Not me. I was going back to Ft. Benning. The 10th Aviation Group at Ft. Benning was organizing and training company size units for deployment to Vietnam. I was being assigned to a newly activated CH-47 medium lift helicopter company that would deploy after it was fully staffed, equipped, and trained. The commander of this company would be LTC Henry (Hank) Moseley. The company was designated the 213th Aviation Assault Support Helicopter Company (ASHC), and LTC Moseley chose the name Black Cats as the unit call sign. Counting the commander, thirty-six aviators would be assigned to the company.

The TOE rank structure of a medium lift helicopter company calls for a major to command, seven company grade commissioned officers, and the remaining rated pilots in the grade of warrant officer. The 213th ASHC would deploy with an unusually high rank structure including one lieutenant colonel, seven majors, and twelve captains; however, a personnel infusion program would be initiated shortly after the 213th ASHC arrived in country. Transferring people in and out of the unit was necessary to sustain a balance of arrivals and departures, evenly spread throughout the year. Without an infusion program, the entire personnel strength of the 213th ASHC would be depleted one year to the day of its arrival. The initial high rank structure would be corrected with the infusion program.

Transition training in the CH-47 was conducted by 10th Aviation Group instructor pilots. After the transition training, most officers were preoccupied with the demanding job of preparing the unit for overseas shipment. The company's aircraft would be flown to Oakland and carried to Vietnam aboard the USNS *Kula Gulf* moored at Alameda Naval Air Station. All company general cargo would be packed in conex containers and shipped from Savannah, Georgia.

Except for the advanced party and a few personnel accompanying cargo aircraft, the main body would be flown by Air Force C-141 aircraft non-stop from Ft. Benning, Georgia to Saigon, Vietnam. Our deployment would be completed by the January 30, 1967. I had finally become a part of the Vietnam troop build-up.

Rally Support Vietnam Personnel
RSVP

During my previous tour at Ft. Benning I had attended the Rotary Wing Instrument Course at Ft. Rucker. This paid unforeseen dividends after I completed my CH-47 qualification training. Only a handful of the thirty-six aviators assigned to our unit were rotary wing instrument qualified. After I was qualified in the CH-47, my company commander gave me the job of conducting a basic rotary wing instrument course to familiarize and instrument qualify as many aviators as I could. This task did two things. First it gave me a lot of flying time in the CH-47. As each day passed, I was becoming the most experienced CH-47 pilot in our new unit. Second, my involvement in training others to fly the CH-47 under instrument conditions released me from the tedious and mundane job of packing equipment for shipment.

One of the captains assigned to the 213th hailed from Columbia, South Carolina. Columbia, the home of Ft. Jackson, had a program in 1966 and 1967 called Rally Support Vietnam Personnel (RSVP) to show its support of the war effort. The mayor of Columbia, Mayor Bates, learned that the 213th ASHC would soon be deploying to Vietnam and that one of Columbia's native sons would be riding along. He sent a letter to LTC Moseley announcing that the Black Cats were being recognized as one of Columbia's RSVP units and invited all or a contingent of the unit to visit Columbia on a football weekend. Colonel Moseley opted for the contingent, sending two aircraft with about ten officers and twenty enlisted men.

Since I was now one of the most experienced CH-47 pilots, I was selected to pilot one of the aircraft. Several city officials were at the Columbia airport to meet us when we landed our two Chinooks. Police officers on motorcycles escorted our drive to a downtown hotel, where we stayed as guests of Mayor Bates and the city of Columbia. Later the same motorcycles led our motorcade to the

University of South Carolina football stadium, where we watched the Gamecocks play the Wildcats of Kentucky. At half-time we were even introduced as the Black Cats who were on their way to "mix it up" in Vietnam. We met Mayor Bates that evening at a dinner that was given in our honor. I will never forget the feelings of pride and gratitude that our entire group felt throughout our visit to Columbia. Columbia had truly rallied our spirits, and we were pumped.

The following day we slept in, toured Columbia, and generally goofed off to give Columbia's native son, now a Vietnam bound Black Cat, some bonus time with his family and friends. Later in the afternoon we assembled at Columbia's Metropolitan Airport for our return trip to Ft. Benning. We had come prepared to give some kind of CH-47 demonstration. We brought sling equipment and nets to carry cargo, and a Chinook's maximum performance takeoff with its mind-boggling rate of ascent is always impressive—but the Blue Angels and the Thunderbirds, we are not. We wanted to impress those who had so impressed us during our visit. I do not know if we did or not, but I do remember that we were rewarded with a couple truck loads of electric fans, portable refrigerators, ice coolers, and window air conditioners. Such a show of gratitude would help alleviate some of the disgust of anti-war demonstrations and Jane Fonda type escapades that uniformed defenders of freedom would soon begin experiencing.

Another Flying *Faux Pas*!

In flying there are cheap lessons learned and expensive lessons learned. A cheap lesson learned cost little more than losing pride and finding embarrassment. An expensive lesson often has dire consequences. Fortunately I avoided the expensive lessons learned, but I seemed to have more than my fair share of the cheap ones.

One such *faux pas* occurred on our return trip to Ft. Benning after the RSVP weekend at Columbia. I had filed a VFR flight plan and would lead our flight of two with a fuel stop at Augusta Regional Airport, also called Bush Field. Ft. Gordon maintains a flight detachment at Bush Field where we would refuel. It was a beautiful, clear night for VFR flying, yet as we approached Augusta, neither my co-pilot nor I could visually find Bush Field. So, I said, "Forget it, we will shoot a VOR instrument approach." I contacted the other aircraft and told them of our intentions and to just follow my lead. After contacting Bush Tower and requesting a VOR approach for our flight of two Chinooks, I quickly glanced at the Bush Field VOR approach plate. I noted that the long final approach leg after passing over the VOR would require a four-minute flight to touchdown at our approach speed.

In less than a minute after passing the VOR, a lighted runway appeared right off our nose. I was just commenting to my co-pilot that we must have one heck of a tail wind when Bush Tower contacted me and asked for my present location. I responded that I had the field in site and that our flight of two was on final approach. Bush tower came back with something like, "I don't think so. I believe you are landing at Daniel Field; maintain present heading and altitude to land at Bush Field!"

A review of the map and the approach plate after landing revealed that Daniel Field was exactly halfway between the VOR and Bush Field, and the final approach radial to Bush Field carried you directly over Daniel Field. Never mind that many other pilots had made the same mistake, I thought it would be a virtual certainty that I would get a merciless razzing when I got back home. After all my counterparts were doing the mundane jobs of packing for deployment while I was flying abundantly in the aircraft with which they were going to war.

I did hear someone say, "Some instrument pilot you are...landing at the wrong field!" Two things helped me. First, shortly after my faux pas, there was a published piece in the paper that reported an incident involving a well-known commercial passenger airliner that apparently did the same thing I did but, embarrassingly, took its passengers all the way to *terra firma* at Daniel rather than Bush Field. The other savior involved the numbers of pilots I was getting rotary wing instrument qualified. This in itself may have precluded some of those expensive lessons learned later in Vietnam, as its weather can be pretty pilot unfriendly, especially around monsoon season.

It's *Deja Vu* All Over Again!

I would, almost four and one-half years after my first helicopter trip to Oakland, California, be winging my way back there again. My flight to the Cities on the Bay this time would also be in a tandem rotor, medium lift helicopter. Turbines had replaced pistons, and, unlike my first trip, in less than forty-five days I would be reunited in South Vietnam with the very aircraft I was piloting. We departed Ft. Benning with a flight of five aircraft and would RON (remain over night) at El Paso and Phoenix along our planned route. We took the southern route to California to avoid the mountains. The remaining thirteen aircraft in our unit would follow the same route to Alemeda, where the aircraft would be prepared for shipment on an aircraft carrier.

The Chinook is a beautiful aircraft to fly. It's cruise speed of 130 knots was the fastest among rotary wing aircraft in 1966. Of course it wasn't designed for hauling passengers on cross country flights. Its fuel capacity would keep its rotors turning for two hours and a few minutes whether you were hovering, lifting and hauling cargo, or just flying cross-country at stretches of about 250 miles between service stations. The trip from Georgia to California had a lot of pit stops, but the speed and the altitude also gave you an aerial view of one great big beautiful country. Perhaps it's the experience that everyone should have before going away to defend their country.

I have nothing racy to report about my graduate journey to Oakland, nothing to equal the undergraduate experience anyway, but our expeditionary incursion into the border town of Juarez, Mexico, was certainly more frivolous than the encounters we would be having with other non-English speaking peoples in the months to come. I also had a lesson learned with charge cards. In those days I was a member of the Playboy Club and was aware that a club had recently opened in Phoenix. Several pilots and I went there for dinner and a show. The entertainment was so good that we decided to stay for the second show. I remember the comedian commenting, "Oh hell, same audience...I'm going to have to change the act!" And he did. I put all charges on my tab. We had such a good time at the Phoenix club that we decided to do the San Francisco Playboy Club as well. I also did a repeat performance with my charge card, a key in those days. And while the guys settled their debts with me, receiving the bill later in Vietnam was not entertaining in the least. We were paid a combat pay supplement of a little over a hundred dollars a month. I can tell you that the Playboy bill was large enough to consume the first few months of combat pay—an expensive lesson learned!

Leaving on a Jet Plane

On January 24, 1967, I assembled with eleven officers and eighty-five enlisted men on Fort Benning's Lawson Army Airfield tarmac to board a huge Air Force C-141 Starlifter that would carry us halfway around the world non-stop to Saigon, Vietnam. Another Starlifter had departed the previous day with the first contingent of the main body. A day before that, two C-130 and one C-141 departed with almost one hundred thousand pounds of TAT (To Accompany Troops) cargo. The company's general cargo had departed Savannah aboard the USS *Defender* on January 2, 1967.

Even today, my thoughts wander back to that cold night in Georgia when I hear the song, "Leaving on a Jet Plan," by Peter, Paul, and Mary. Our Starlifter ride was hardly a good experience. The night of our departure was one of those rare freezing nights in South Georgia, and it remained uncomfortable during the next sixteen hours as we crossed the northern and western hemispheres via the polar route. We were seated in troop seats along both sides of the fuselage with our personal gear and TOE equipment strapped to the floor in front of us. This would be a godsend as it provided a place to elevate feet and keep them off the floor that was cold enough to freeze spilled coffee. And, oh yes, you can always tell you're flying economy/coach class when there aren't any windows. The flight seemed like a short tour in itself, but eventually we did arrive at Ton San Nhut Airport, Saigon, Vietnam.

NFGs at Last

Members of our advanced party met us at Ton San Nhut, and after off-loading personal gear from the airplane and on-loading it into trucks, we departed by motor vehicle convoy for Phu Loi. The aviation elements already at Phu Loi included the Headquarters, 11th Combat Aviation Battalion, our parent unit, oursister units, the 128th Assault Helicopter Company, the 205th Assault Support Helicopter Company, and the 21st Aviation Reconnaissance Company. It was also the home of Headquarters, 1st Infantry Division Artillery, the 1st Squadron, 4th Cavalry of the 1st Division, and the 168th Engineer Battalion. The 213th had been allotted a nine and one-half acre area with seven permanent structures. We were moving into an area formerly occupied by another Chinook Company, the 178th ASHC.

Our new home, Phu Loi Airfield, was about twenty-five or so miles due north of Saigon. The airfield had been used by the Japanese during the Second World War. American POWs in that era had helped clear the jungle and level the landing surface for Japanese fighter planes. The runway in 1967 was 2900 feet of PSP (pierced steel plate) platform. The defense perimeter around the airfield was triangular shaped, each side less than one mile in length, and with artillery units located in each of the three vertices.

The USNS *Kula Gulf* arrived at Vung Tau, an eastern coastal city about seventy-five miles due east of Phu Loi, on January 29. The general cargo, that had departed by ship from Savannah, Georgia, arrived at Phu Loi by motor vehicle convoy during the first week in February. The last of our eighteen CH-47A aircraft also arrived at Phu Loi by the end of the first week in February, 1967. As all of us have experienced, unpacking is always easier than packing. The 213th ASHC Black Cats were ready to start weighing-in for the war effort.

Home Sweet Home

Our arrival at our Phu Loi homestead was a pleasant surprise. The advance party had organized the area quite well in short order. The entire unit would be housed in permanent buildings with metal roofs overhead. The pilots would occupy an elongated structure that looked like an old motel. We called it the Bates Motel, the famed motel in the movie, *Psycho*. The Bates Motel had ten to twelve doors facing to the front of the building, each providing private entrances to an individual room that could accommodate from two to four people. I shared a two-man room with another captain. Each room had its own wash basin and electrical outlet for appliances. A separate community shower facility and latrine were designated for just the occupants of the Bates Motel. Electrical power was provided by the Phu Loi base engineer, so electric fans, small refrigerators, radios, tape recorders, and even small air conditioners could be used. The company had backup generators in case of power outages, which were fairly infrequent. We would share the consolidated mess hall with all 11th Battalion aviation units at Phu Loi. The 11th Battalion even had its own officer club, non-commission officer's club, and enlisted club as well. One could not help noticing the swimming pool and tennis court that we passed as we walked from the 213th ASHC and the 11th Battalion consolidated mess hall. All in all it was pretty plush living for the combat zone.

One of the things that I would bet everyone included early on in their first letters home was a comment regarding the deafening decibels that were undoubtedly disturbing their nocturnal dozing. Trying to sleep with 105 mm and 155 mm howitzers firing away indiscriminately throughout the night takes a little getting used to. The artillerymen called their mission harassment and interdiction fire. For the first few nights you wondered, *who in the world are they trying to harass— me*? Like all things in life, one adapts, and before long you begin to start sleeping like a baby. The booming artillery then becomes sort of your security blanket—that is, as long as the booming is outbound. The inbound booming is another story that comes later.

In-Country Training

Our CH-47 training at Ft. Benning had taught us most of the skills that we would need in order to support our field units in Vietnam. We had practiced moving 105 mm howitzers together with their trailing piggyback netted loads of ammunition and every conceivable type of cargo that we might expect to be carrying in our operational area (AO) of Vietnam. Getting familiar with the lay of the land, the radio contacts and procedures, and how the CH-47 were to be employed by the various major supported units (25th Infantry Division, 1st Infantry Division, and 9th Infantry Division) was something that would require time and experience. This flying time and experience would be provided initially by our sister unit at Phu Loi, the 205th ASHC Geronimos.

The thing I remember most about my training with the 205th was not the flying in the field. In my two or three week in-country train-up, I cannot recall a single incident that would have led me to believe that we were flying over a hostile environment. That would come later. What comes to mind is the contraption that was rigged in all the Geronimo aircrafts' cockpits to give armament protection to pilots. Body armor vests were available in 1967, but not yet in the 205th ASHC. When flying a Geronimo CH-47, you climbed into a comfortable pilot's seat, then locked yourself into a bullet proof, rectangular shaped box. The armament cumbrously surrounded you with arm openings to access the flight controls. It was the Rube Goldberg of Rube Goldbergs. The body armor vests that we would soon be wearing in our Black Cat aircraft were dubbed "chicken plates." The Geronimo pilots used such unaffectionate names as "the chastity belt" or "the cockpit coffin" to describe their protective armament.

The first lesson one learns in Vietnam is that you are essentially out of small arms range when you climb through two thousand feet; so you learn real fast that two thousand feet and higher is a popular flight level for most chopper pilots. What goes up, however, must come down, and that's where vulnerability comes into play. Besides the possibility of becoming a target, flying in Vietnam was challenging in other respects. The hot and humid temperature, the inclement weather that always accompanies the monsoon season, the dust and debris forever present in hastily prepared landing zones, and the sheer number of flying hours one could expect to fly from dawn to dusk were among the contrasts to stateside flying. During those early days of our training with the 205th, I remember leaving the aircraft absolutely beat at day's end. No doubt some of that fatigue was caused by stress, but flying eight to twelve hours in one day entails perhaps as many as thirty to fifty landings. I remember writing home and describing my experience scooting around in Vietnam airspace as a great big flying sauna. My sweat glands were getting a real workout.

Duty, Honor, Company

As mentioned earlier, a lieutenant colonel was assigned as the commanding officer of the newly constituted 213th, and he would soon be joined by the assignment of seven majors and a dozen or so company grade officers. Being rank heavy in the initial stages of unit formation and preparation for overseas deployment has its obvious advantages, but the 213th's officer structure was the antithesis of what an ASHC TOE should look like. While the infusion program would take care of the rank structure imbalance in time, the initial duty assignments for company grade officers, like myself, would certainly not tax leadership skills. Since I was a relatively junior among my company grade peers, the only thing I would ever command in the 213th was the aircraft we flew. I was selected to be an Aircraft Commander (AC) because I had the most flying hours and experience in the CH-47 due to my instrument flying instruction back at Ft. Benning.

My assigned jobs were safety officer and instrument instructor pilot. I also taught the pilots how to use a British air-navigation system called Decca. Decca pinpointed a pilot's position and tracked his flight on a scrolled 1:50,000 map displayed within the cockpit. Potentially the Decca system had great utility as a navigational aid, but pilots preferred marrying eyeballs with maps, and consequently, the Decca system never became too popular and was seldom used.

I did take my job as safety officer very seriously and strived to promote safe flying practices in our company by making our unit safety meetings as informative, interesting, and mission oriented as possible. To this end I had guest speakers from other units and services such as Pathfinders and Riggers, Boeing Vertol representatives, Air Traffic Controllers, and Fire Support Coordinators.

The value of having these guests became readily apparent to all of us one night about three months into our tour. The 205th had taught us how to check active artillery firing, throughout the III Corps AO.

70

It was a simple enough procedure as all airfields and major installations had a published frequency that provided, upon request, vectors of active artillery fire from that installation. We had assumed that the installation's report included all types of artillery firing but learned from our Fire Support Coordinator guest that only 155 mm and 175 mm artillery was reported. Somebody said, "How about 105 mm?" The negative response to the question was a positive learning experience for all. You can be sure that everyone began to inquire further about 105 mm firing while flying in the AO.

We also learned from Saigon ATC, called Paris Control, what services they could provide. Before the visit nobody even contacted Paris Control. After the visit many, including myself, used Paris Control to obtain radar vectors for navigational purposes.

The following pictures show a Chinook that hit by a 105 mm round yet survived to fly another day. This incident actually occurred during my second tour. In this case the projectile did not detonate, it just happened to be passing through! The round punctured the fuel cell, severed several hydraulic lines, and exited through the fuselage on the opposite side of the aircraft. Some of the hydraulic fluid and JP4 was sucked into the exhaust, causing what appeared to be a huge flaming afterburner from the right engine. The pilot shut down the burning engine and safely landed the aircraft.

A "friendly fire" 105mm round registers a direct hit on a CH-47. The round punctures the fuel cell.

The round exits the aircraft without detonating, Thank God!

Being Safety Officer Has Its Perks

After my in-country CH-47 check out, I was informed that I would attend a week long Jungle Environmental Survival Training (JEST) course at Subic Bay in the Philippines. Each company in the 11th Combat Aviation Battalion would send one pilot, ideally the safety officer, so that he could teach what he had learned upon returning to his home unit. The USN sponsored JEST course was designed to teach pilot's jungle survival skills and escape and evasion tactics. Among the cadre were indigenous Negritos (my instructor had been a scout for the U.S. Army during WWII) who taught us everything we wanted to know about edible plants and where to find water vines. I had sampled the local beer, San Miguel, in the Clark Air Base Officers Open Mess (CABOOM) club the day before with my Air Force, Navy, and Army JEST classmates. It was decided then that nobody in his right mind would go voluntarily into the jungle without a good supply of pilsner provisions. We loaded our duffels with San Miguel. And so, my first joint service school experience would not be unlike the one I would encounter four years later at the Armed Forces Staff College.

Infusion and Confusion

The infusion effort started soon after we arrived in-country. One of the early transfers was the commander, Lieutenant Colonel Moseley, who was replaced by his executive officer, Major George "Wally" Adamson. Without an infusion program, the 213th, with a strength of 225 enlisted and 36 officers would DEROS exactly twelve months from the day of arrival, leaving eighteen pilotless CH-47 helicopters and nary a sole to maintain them. The task of ensuring that you had sustainable balance of personnel gains and losses each and every month was especially difficult in the early months. The mastermind behind this undertaking had to be a diplomat, a master of organization, a superb communicator, and downright smart. I would bet my bottom dollar that the very man who was responsible for contriving the year long infusion plan was a guy named Wally.

During the early months of 1967, Major Adamson came up with an ingenious idea that should have earned him an impact award from the Deputy Chief of Staff for Personnel at the Department of the Army. The Aviation Schools' output of pilots and aircraft mechanics could not keep pace with the demands of the field. The turnaround time between first and second short-tours to Vietnam in the late sixties was about eighteen, max twenty-four months, and it seemed to be diminishing by the month. Maintenance supervisors' stateside R&Rs were even more abbreviated. The Army was seeking ways and means to extend the turnaround time using the reenlistment bonus as its primary incentive.

Wally Adamson used a different approach—one that would benefit the Black Cats and the Army as well. Major Adamson announced, in writing, that anybody who extended his tour for six additional months would stay with the Black Cats for his entire tour. Now remember, we were all together at Ft. Benning for at least six months.

And also remember that our accommodations at Phu Loi were not too shabby. The Wallygram caught everyone's attention, big time.

It had indeed caught the attention of one maintenance supervisor who thought it might be one of those decisions that he should run by the boss who was running his family operation stateside. Her response was pithy and to the point. She said, "I'm going to be doing a whole lot of fucking on or about 25 January 1968, and if you want to be a part of it, you had better be here!" The maintenance supervisor showed his wife's letter to his commander, Major Adamson, and guess what? Major Adamson had a sense of humor and smarts too. The maintenance supervisor stayed in the unit, *sans* extension, and got a piece of the action on or about 25 January 1968 as well.

Captain Underpants to the Rescue

I have never met a Mormon that I didn't like. My roommate was no exception, but as I staggered in from my days flying and watched him do likewise, I could not help but noticing something that I thought real strange. We were in a tropical climate, had to wear flight suits made of a heavy fire retardant fabric called nomex, and my roommate was wearing long johns. After some joking about not looking cool in long johns, I reminded him that the supply room was giving away free olive drab GI underwear and suggested he go get some. The next time I saw the long johns under his flight suit, I decided to do something cool for him. I picked him up about a half-dozen pair of skivvies and brought them back to the room and threw them on his bunk where he was reading. I knew from the expression on his face when he saw them flying his way that I had done stepped on my poncho. He told me something about his faith and beliefs that I do not remember. The Lord sure works in mysterious ways.

Hot LZ

My baptism by fire came during early February, 1967, in a landing zone just north of Nui Ba Den, that lonesome mountain northeast of Tay Ninh. We were supporting the insertion of 25th Infantry troops into an LZ that had not been prepped with artillery. The ground commander was relying on the element of surprise I suppose, but obviously, the surprise insertion on this operation would backfire for the good guys. Airmobile operations, when properly executed, are a beautiful thing to watch. The timed artillery prep pounds the LZ while the troop loaded slicks are airborne and en route. The gunships leading the troop carriers close toward the LZ and begin firing their ordinance just as the artillery signals its last volley with two Willey Pete (white phosphorous) rounds. The slicks touchdown with the door gunners blazing and the gunships raking the LZ perimeter. It's like watching a well-executed touchdown play at a football game. But on this February day of 1967 there would be a busted play.

Our mission was to fly in the 105 mm howitzers to the LZ, concurrently with the first insertion of infantry. The very howitzers that should have been pounding the LZ were airborne, being carried by slings below our Chinooks with the gun crews riding with us. Before the LZ was even in sight, I knew things were not going well by the radio traffic. A Huey had been hit on the ground and was burning. About the same time I was hearing this radio transmission, the LZ came into sight and so did the burning Huey. I saw not only a burning Huey but a burning body running, then falling near his aircraft. Our attention now was solely directed to the pathfinder who was popping smoke for the point on the ground where he wanted the artillery piece I was carrying.

The pathfinder radioed that he suspected command detonated mines and that our designated landing area was clear. My approach into his designated cleared area was almost vertically straight down

Hueys on their approach. For some it would be their final approach.

Landing and lending firepower for the battlefield.

from about two hundred feet. We landed the howitzer, together with its piggyback ammo load, then discharged the gun crew. As we were departing I saw another Hucy get hit in the tail boom near the tail rotor. He was low enough to make a controlled crash, but the projectile that hit the ship was certainly not a command detonated mine; it was probably a RPG (rocket propelled grenade). I reported what I had observed to the pathfinder who directed our landing and the positioning of the howitzer.

From the radio traffic I was monitoring I knew that Tac Air was on the way, and unfortunately, so too was dustoff aircraft. Our flight of five Chinooks departed safely from the LZ after landing a battery of howitzers that were undoubtedly put into service in short order. We flew back to the staging area at Tay Ninh and checked our aircraft for damage. We found some bullet holes but nothing that would require more than minor sheet metal repair. We performed no more sorties to that LZ and eventually flew off to other missions within our AO. I never heard about the outcome of that particular battle. We supported three Infantry Divisions and went from one unit to the next, giving support when and where it was needed. It was that way throughout this tour, but this was my first experience and that's probably why I recall it so vividly, even after thirty-five years.

Black Hat Pathfinder has marked gun position with smoke. This picture, taken through the CH-47 undercarriage opening, directly above the hook, shows a howitzer being lowered to spot where the pathfinder wants it.

Party Time

"There is nothing like a dame, nothing in the world." So go the lyrics to that upbeat song in the musical, *South Pacific*. The GI sentiment toward the female gender two wars later had not changed. Vietnam too had its share of head turners. They were affiliated with the USO, Special Services, Red Cross, Military Nurse Corps, and Civil Service in countless U.S. government agencies. Many frequently visited field units by chopper, resulting in acquaintances and friendships between pilots and passengers. Somebody during the spring of 1967 in the 11th Combat Aviation Battalion, suggested it was time to show our in-country feminine friends some classy appreciation for their support and presence in the war zone.

Once it was decided the party was a go, good old American GI ingenuity was set into motion. Unlike the story in Tour One (Korea), which recounted how grunts succeeded in bird dogging Red Legs by shanghaiing their Round Eyes, this event would be staged with as much pizzazz as we could possibly muster in our olive drab environment. Hors d'oeuvres and cocktails would precede a pool side dinner party. A live band and a floor show would provide the entertainment. Transportation to and from the party would be by helicopter. Use of the Chinook was discussed for the larger parties of guests coming out of Saigon and Long Bien.

For anyone who has flown as a passenger in a Chinook, you can appreciate the understatement that there are better ways to travel. Cargo trucks like those used in the Korea Round Eye heist might have been even more comfortable. Somebody got the ingenious idea to construct a pod that could be inserted into the Chinook's fuselage, making it a stretch airborne limousine of sorts. A sound insulated plywood pod was constructed, complete with a bar, Chinook pilot seats (every bit as comfortable as your recliner at home), air conditioning, and an in-flight music system. A tuxedo clad steward served libations and edibles during the flight. It was a champagne flight probably unequaled anytime and anywhere by a combat support aircraft during the Vietnam War.

The evening was perfect for a pool party. The pool was lit with tiki torches, and all of our lovely guests were given a lei as a welcome gesture. The party was a huge success, and somewhere, even after some thirty-five years, I know there are thirty or forty women that would smilingly concur. On that night we made everyone of them feel like, "There is nothing like a dame, nothing in the world."

The 3 Zulu Learning Curve

I had been with the Black Cats for about six months when I was told that I would be reassigned to our battalion headquarters and would be working in the S-3 shop. The infusion program was alive and well, and it was serving me well. The battalion S-3 was LTC Jim Patterson, who had been awarded our country's second highest award for valor, the Distinguished Service Cross, while commanding the 216th AHC just prior to becoming the 11th CAB S-3. Later, after a distinguished career, Jim Patterson would become a major general. As his assistant S-3 (with my call sign, 3 Zulu), I would learn many valuable lessons about planning and executing air-mobile operations. One of my primary functions would be to manipulate available battalion aircraft assets and cross reinforce units to insure that all commitments were successfully completed. As 3 Zulu, I would face such emergencies as aircraft shot down in hostile territory, aircraft accidents, missing aircraft, and enemy mortar and rocket attacks of battalion units. Lessons learned during this assignment would prove invaluable during my subsequent tour where I would become the S 3 of the 11th Aviation Group of the 1st Air Cavalry Division, the Army's largest single aviation unit in Vietnam with over 425 assigned helicopters.

The Headquarters, 11th Combat Aviation Battalion (CAB), a unit within the 1st Aviation Brigade, had three Assault Support Helicopter Companies (128th AHC, 162nd AHC, and the 173rd AHC), two Assault Support Helicopter Companies (205th ASHC and 213th ASHC), and one Reconnaissance Airplane Company (21st RAC). Four of the 11th CAB companies, the 128th, 205th, 213th and 21st, were located with the battalion headquarters at Phu Loi. The 162nd was located at Phuoc Vinh, some 20-25 miles north of Phu Loi. The 173rd's home was Lai Khe, also about 20 miles north of Phu Loi, but west of Phuoc Vinh. With approximately 150 aircraft, the 11th CAB's mission was to support the three Infantry Divisions (1st, 9th, and

25th) that were operating in the III Corps area of operations (AO). The daily sorties to support this mission were many and varied.

I reported for duty well versed in Chinook operations but lacked experience in air assault and troop lift tactics and procedures. Therefore, I flew just as often as possible with the 128th AHC during troop combat assaults. After several missions, both in slicks and gunships, I started flying Smokey, a Huey that produced a smoke screen to obscure a selected segment of the assault LZ in order to cover our aircraft and troops while landing. One of the most important lessons I learned during my 3 Zulu assignment was that commanders and operation officers need to be where the troop support they are responsible for is being rendered. Every 11th CAB commander and operations officer I observed during my tenure as 3 Zulu was where the action was. That lesson learned as a 3 Zulu in the 11th CAB would become my creed when I took my turn in the barrel as a commander and S-3 during my second tour in Vietnam.

My 3 Zulu job gave me the opportunity to work with many of the real pioneers in Army aviation. One of those people, the commander of the 11th Combat Aviation Battalion, Colonel Leo Soucek, would also be the commander of the 11th Aviation Group, First Air Cavalry Division, when I reported to begin my second tour of duty in Vietnam. Colonel Soucek would give me the opportunity to command an aviation unit in combat.

R & R

If you polled every Vietnam veteran to determine the most favorite acronym among the twenty trillion that must have existed, the number one acronym would be DEROS. Right on its tail, however, would have to be R&R. R&Rs were popular—and why not? Imagine yourself in your current job selecting where you would like to vacation (air fare paid), anywhere in the northern and western hemisphere. That's what we had back when we worked for Uncle Sam in Vietnam. We could go to some of the most exotic destinations within the northern and eastern hemispheres. You name it—Tokyo, Hong Kong, Bangkok, Seoul, Kwala Lampur, and Tai Pei. We could even slip down under to Australia, but the most popular R&R site, especially for the married service members, was Hawaii. The shortest week in one's short tour occurred when you left your place of peril, traveling and enjoying seven days and six nights in paradise, then returned again to your place of peril. Time between perils seemed to be all of ten minutes when you view it in the wake.

My R&R to Hawaii in 1967 was most memorable. I was flown to Ton Son Khut the evening before my departure, spent the evening at the base BOQ, then reported the next morning to the R&R Center with about a hundred other excited guys who were assembling to board a commercial 707 jet for our twelve hour non-stop flight to Honolulu. Soldiers from all four Corps areas were assembling for the trip. I looked around to see if I recognized anyone and was pleasantly surprised to see one of my best friends, Tom Wolf, whom I had served with during my assignment with the 2nd Aviation Battalion at Ft. Benning. Our families had spent an entire summer together during a TDY trip to the U.S. Military Academy where Tom and I flew CH-34s in support of cadet summer training. We even rented from the same people, a military couple who owned a large farmhouse outside Cornwall, New York, and experienced communal living of sorts.

It was a fortuitous coincidence that we should be on the same R&R flight and it was great too because we were all such good friends.

But then Tom, who must have been producing testosterone at unprecedented levels, began to worry that the Lanzotti's presence would interfere with his longed dreamed-about solitude with his wife. Kiddingly, I think, he kept warning and threatening me with such tripe as, "Lanzotti, I don't want to hear from you for three days after we arrive!" He even told me that if his wife wanted to see the island, he would oblige her by moving the bed closer to the window. Tom's imagination would soon be competing with his stamina.

Our wives, who were waiting for our arrival at the Honolulu Airport, had the same surprising reunion as Tom and I had experienced just a few hours earlier. After exchanging hotel names and numbers we departed without any plans to get together, but that would certainly take place once Tom's appetite for intimacy had been satisfied. Less than one hour after checking into our room, the telephone rang. It was Tom asking, "What are you guys doing dinner tonight?" So much for Tom's imagination—and stamina!

Thousands upon thousands of men and women in uniform were flown to Hawaii during the Vietnam era. As a tribute to the most popular military R&R location on this planet, the Hale Koa Hotel, at Ft. DeRussy, was opened for business in 1975. Today the Hale Koa, with 817 rooms, occupies sixty-six acres right smack dab in the middle of Waikiki Beach. Its mission, "To provide a first class hotel and recreational facility at affordable prices for military members and their families," is being superbly accomplished 7/24/365. It's truly a world class hotel, and if you're active or retired military and haven't been there, you need to treat yourself and your family to a super R&R.

Fruitcakes and Patriotism

Any helicopter pilot who ever flew ash and trash sorties or mail run missions to field units in Vietnam during the Christmas season of 1967 would question if the world would ever run out of fruitcakes. Our helicopters literally hauled tons and tons of fruitcakes in 1967. Prior holiday seasons were no different except perhaps the tonnage was slightly less because the peak troop build up had not yet been achieved. It was as if everyone in America thought that a fruitcake was the perfect gift to show their support for uniformed men and women fighting for their country overseas. Already preserved and packed, it was an easy gift to send in the mail. The thought and support was evident, and that was the most important gift of all.

The reason I mention this piece of trivia is that my second tour to Vietnam, just two holiday seasons later, would be noticeably different. In 1969, the fruitcakes had all but vanished, and with them so had the support of the people back home. Is it silly to make a correlation between fruitcakes and patriotism? To me it's as serious as a heart beat. Fighting a war without fruitcakes is like playing on a team without fans. Unfortunately, most of the fruitcakes during the 1970 holiday season were protesting and demonstrating in American streets. I would hope we never see that kind of behavior again. I would also hope that we as a nation have learned the lesson to always support, no matter how protracted, those who make the sacrifices to defend our country's freedoms. Praise the Lord and keep them fruitcakes coming.

Incoming

If you have ever been on the receiving end of a NVA mortar or rocket attack, you can appreciate what effect our artillery has on those who just unfortunately might be occupying the planned LZ we selected for an air assault and insertion of troops. As a slick pilot, it's very comforting to see friendly artillery pounding the LZ just seconds before you touch down. Likewise, it's a nice feeling to see gunships in front of you strafing with mini-guns and firing salvos of 2.75 inch rockets. My experience on the receiving end of enemy incoming was frightening enough. Nobody had to encourage me to find cover and keep my head down, but all of the incoming I experienced was in a fire support base and was never concentrated, nor in the volume that bombarded a LZ. That's why I always felt comfortable when I flew air assaults, either as a slick pilot or while flying Smokey, to lay down a protective smoke screen for the troops we were inserting. The amount of fire directed to where I was intending to be was enough to keep the bad guys head down long enough for me to do what I came to do.

During my tenure as 3 Zulu, I had several experiences with incoming. Typically the enemy mortar attacks on Phu Loi were sporadic and ineffective, unlike our unit at Phouc Vinh, the 162nd AHC, which seemed to be on the receiving end almost every night. I remember saying over and over again, "God, I would hate to be living at Phuoc Vinh!" One night, however, the enemy added 122mm rockets to its mortar attack on Phu Loi, the first time that I had experienced the incoming rockets. There were some hits on aircraft on our flight line. The attack did not last long, but this one had been effective. My job as 3 Zulu was to scramble gunships to try to find the enemy gunners. Usually that call wasn't necessary as the gunships had already launched and were searching.

An incoming story that I have told over and over involved a very likable S-2 major on our staff. The night of the big rocket attack on

Phu Loi was within a week of his DEROS and he was celebrating. It had to be some pretty heavy celebrating, because somehow he had slept right through the incoming rockets that were slamming into our battalion area. Anyway, when incoming is detected, a siren alarm is sounded and everyone scurries for cover, then a few minutes after the last round impacts, the siren is sounded again to signal all-clear.

About one minute after sounding the all-clear siren, our S-2 staggers into the ops bunker wearing nothing but a steel pot, flack jacket, and skivvies, and says, "Another god-damned practice alert?" As the S-2 he was responsible for an assigned sector of Phu Loi's guarded perimeter defense and was required to check our guards during both practice alerts as well as real attacks. His grand entrance and his statement were funny enough, but his response to Colonel Soucek—after he was apprised that, no, it was a real attack and he had missed all the fun—was one of the best one liners I have ever heard. Colonel Soucek, who liked this S-2 as if he were a son, discretely filled him in on the known damages and current situation, then said as our S-2 was about to leave, "Jake, take it easy out there and keep your head down." Our S-2 tipped his steel bonnet and said, "Colonel, if I am not back by Easter, go ahead and hide the eggs!"

Smokey

After a few flights with the 128th in their slicks and gunships, I began to fly Smokey, a UH-1 that was configured with an oil pump that directed oil to a ring attached to the engine's exhaust stack. When oil was flushed into the superheated exhaust, it created a white wall of smoke that would obscure the arrival and departure of a C-141 Starlifter. When wind conditions were favorable and a segment of the LZ appeared to provide advantageous fields of fire for the enemy, Smokey was called upon. The 1st Infantry Division was the most frequent user of Smokey. Their employment of Smokey was always prefaced with artillery preps and gunship escorts.

The old adage that "flying helicopters can be hours and hours of boredom, interrupted by moments of stark terror" is as true for me as anyone who has ever flown in a combat environment. I have had my hours and hours of boredom, and I've had a moment or two of terror. One of the latter moments occurred in Smokey while supporting the 25th Infantry Division on a beautiful day in the late fall of 1967. I was flying with a friend, Steve Stout (later a Pam Am pilot I believe), and we were laying a smoke screen along the north side of a number of elongated villages between Cu Chi and Tay Ninh. The plan was to obscure the landing of our helicopters and allow the landed troops to sweep the village. The pickup was accomplished after the sweep without Smokey, as the village was deemed clear.

It was about the third village that all hell broke loose. We laid our landing zone smoke screen without incident, the infantry swept the village, but when the first couple of helicopters touched down, they were taken under fire. The fire was coming from the village they had just cleared! Two choppers were hit as they touched down. One was able to fly away, but one was disabled and was being pounded by automatic fire coming from the village. We could see the rounds hitting the standing water in the rice fields where the infantry was pinned down. We started to see mortar rounds hitting the pickup zone. I remember Steve saying, It's show time! I was flying, and we knew that we needed to put a smoke screen between the village and the pinned down infantry so that other orbiting helicopters could land and safely extract our guys. As we came in low and fast, the bad guys' guns started swinging our way, and I could see the rounds hitting the wet ground in front of us. We put down a beautiful smoke screen that was no doubt even prettier to those hunkered down in the rice paddies as it was to the orbiting aircraft.

Nobody in our aircraft was hurt, and we could find only a couple of bullet holes in the aircraft. When we were on the ground inspecting the aircraft for damage, Steve said to me, "Bob, I think you were trying to hide behind that cyclic, and if the red trim button was an olive, the pimento would be propelled right through the cockpit's roof!" I was indeed leaning forward into that cyclic. I think I was trying to climb all of me into my armament chest protector, and I know those knuckles gripping that cyclic were mighty white! After the troops were safely extracted, Steve and I witnessed the disappearance of that village by our supporting artillery. In retrospect those were some of the moments that punctuated those many hours of boredom. That day Steve and I had earned our salary and the appreciation of many that we did not know and would never see again.

Leaving on a Jet Plane

My DEROS was on January 25, 1968, and I was leaving on a jet plane from Ben Hoa. I had almost frozen to death on my C-141 trip from Ft. Benning to Ton Son Nhut. My departure from Ben Hoa just one year later would become the antithesis to that experience.

I boarded the 707 commercial jet, and it taxied to the runway where we sat for almost two hours without air-conditioning. Initially I thought it might be an air traffic control glitch, but as time went on I began to think that it had to be a mechanical problem and repairs were being made, although nobody could see anyone working on the airplane. The pilots were not telling us anything other than intermittent announcements that there would be a further delay of just a few more minutes. After an hour the temperature inside the airplane was about as hot as the surface of the tarmac outside. Everyone was drenched with sweat. When at last we began our takeoff roll, everyone cheered, then quickly cringed as the aircraft seemed to be literally yanked off the runway. It was by far the roughest takeoff I have ever experienced on board a commercial carrier.

If the takeoff was bad, it paled compared to the landing to come. The captain announced shortly after takeoff that the routing home would now include a refueling stop at Clark AFB. The landing at Clark was, I think, a controlled crash. The flight attendant could have said, "Welcome to Clark AFB" three or four times, because that's the number of times we bounced and careened down the runway. We deplaned and were told that there could be a slight delay. The slight delay was extended slightly—to three days! A delay of any kind when you are going home to meet loved ones who are waiting for you is catastrophic, but three days!

As it turned out, the plane needed a part that was in Miami, Florida. It was flown to Clark AFB, then repairs were made and the flight continued. The entire manifest of that airplane was pretty pissed off when we finally left Clark AFB, but to the credit of the cockpit crew, the takeoff and landings were good, particularly that one at San Francisco International.

Three days after my arrival the TET Offensive was raging in Vietnam. A coordinated attack with seventy thousand North Vietnamese soldiers was initiated on the night of January 31, 1968. They were attacking throughout South Vietnam, including the U.S. Embassy in Saigon. It was called the turning point of the war. There were over five hundred thousand U.S. military in Vietnam when I left. It was likely that I would be going back soon. The one-half million troop strength would, in fact, continue for another five years after TET, but the maintenance of support from the American people would not be sustained. There was an explosion of dissent that grew with every year after TET of 1968.

A Short Stop Between Short Tours

My new assignment was at the U.S. Army Aviation School Element at Ft. Stewart, Georgia. The turn-around time between my first and second Vietnam tours would be slightly less than eighteen months. At Ft. Stewart I was assigned to the 267th Aviation Battalion, a composite school support battalion, consisting of a reinforced rifle company, an artillery battery, a TDA aviation support company, and headquarters company. I served as CO of the aviation support company and later as the battalion XO. My service in the battalion was really limited to about one year as I attended an eight week Fixed Wing Qualification Course at Ft. Rucker immediately before going on leave prior to my second Vietnam tour. I mention my assignment to Ft. Stewart as it was a challenge in stress almost equaling a combat tour.

Let me explain. It had been almost two years since Secretary McNamara's Project 100,000 was initiated. You might recall that Project 100,000 was DOD's response to President Johnson's War on Poverty. The Project relaxed the aptitude standards for volunteers and draftees all the way down to category four (the thirtieth percentile and lower) of the Armed Forces Qualification Test. Fortunately, there was a proviso in the program that disallowed Project 100,000 recruits from being sent to the combat zone. Good thing. One such soldier in my company purchased a revolver from a local pawn shop, then shot another soldier in his platoon while showing it to him. The wound was not life-threatening, but it was serious. The low aptitude military recruits were limited to 100,000 per year, and it seemed to me that the 267th was getting more than its fair share. Between our assigned Project 100,000 people and the short timers coming back from Vietnam, I learned a whole lot about the Code of Military Justice as well as the names of everyone who worked in the Ft. Stewart JAG office.

My military law schooling didn't last long. I was alerted in the early spring of 1969 that orders were coming. I was being slated to attend the Fixed Wing Qualification Course at Ft. Rucker en route with a reporting date to USARV in late August. I was on my way to my third and final short tour and my second in Vietnam.

Tour Three:

Vietnam 2

My Greatest Army Adventure

My long ride back to Vietnam this time was comfortable and uneventful. The big 707 landed at Ben Hoa, where we were met by a bus and carried to Long Bien for in-processing. I was surprised to see two of my Fixed Wing Qualification Course classmates, also majors, who had arrived for processing earlier in the morning. A personnel specialist announced that he had command assignments for each of us, all at different units. One of us would be going to the 101st, one to the 1st Aviation Brigade, and one to the 1st Cavalry Division. My preference was to go back to the 1st Aviation Brigade. I yearned to command the Tomahawks, the 128th AHC at Phu Loi. My least favorite of the three, at that time, was the 1st Air Cavalry Division. The personnel specialist turned first to Major Grant Green and said, "You are being assigned to the 101st." I did not have to sweat it too long because he announced my assignment next. I would be going to the 1st Cav.

My ride to the 1st Cavalry Division Headquarters would be by helicopter. I had no idea where I was going other than I was being carried to my third choice. The 1st Cav Chinook that picked all of us NFGs up at the Long Bien helipad looked pretty grimy, as if it lived in the field. It landed, dropped its rear ramp, and about thirty new cavalrymen climbed aboard. Our departure from Long Bien was north, and the flight lasted only about twenty minutes.

We landed, the ramp went down, and while exiting the aircraft, I yelled to the crew chief over the din of the engines, "Where are we?" I had to repeat myself, as the crew chief had to remove his helmet. His response was my second nightmare of the morning. He yelled, "You are at the 1st Cav headquarters, Phuoc Vinh, Vietnam!" Phouc Vinh! During the latter months of 1968, the 1st Air Cavalry Division had moved from I Corps to III Corps with the division base established at Phuoc Vinh. After my 3 Zulu experience, if anyone would have asked me where I would not want to be in Vietnam, my response without hesitation would have been Phuoc Vinh. I had just arrived, and already I was a two-time loser.

A jeep was at the airfield to take me to the 11th Aviation Group Headquarters where I was to meet the group commander. I learned from the driver en route that the group commander was Colonel Soucek, the same Soucek I had worked for at the 11th Combat Aviation Battalion less than two years earlier. Things were looking up, for this was the first good news I had gotten all day. Our meeting was cordial, but Colonel Soucek's plans for me did not exactly coincide with what I wanted. I was sure I wanted to command an assault helicopter company in one of his two lift battalions. Colonel Soucek told me that one was not available at present. He would try to satisfy my request, but what he really needed, right away, was a Chinook company commander. Well, what's a guy to do? I replied, "Okay, sir, where and when?"

I was introduced to the 228th Assault Support Battalion commanding officer, LTC Emory Bush, who would, in a little over two years later, become my faculty advisor at the Armed Forces Staff College. Colonel Bush took me to the company that I was going to command, Charlie Company, and introduced me to the current commander. He left us to discuss the company and its mission, aircraft status, and personnel. I learned that the company's call sign was Crimson Tide and I would soon be Tide 6. The three companies in the 228th Assault Support Helicopter Battalion were named after college teams: Longhorns, Wildcats, and Crimson Tide. Being on the Fighting Illini football team during my college days, I was not really too thrilled with my new handle, Tide 6. During the last tour I had witnessed a change of command for the Tomahawks, the 128th AHC at Phu Loi. Watching the outgoing commander remove his Indian war bonnet and place it on the head of the new Tomahawk 6 was a real turn-on for me. I pictured myself, a true Fighting Illini, wearing that war bonnet. Now I was a Crimson Tide, whatever that was.

Settling In

We were looking at the company billet area when the incoming mortar attack began. About a half dozen rounds hit the company area. One unfortunate Charlie company enlisted man was killed by a single piece of shrapnel while standing in the pay line. My thoughts were, naturally, nothing has changed! I would learn, during my next twelve months at Phuoc Vinh, that things do change. That was the last mortar attack to hit our company area for the remainder of my tour. The frequency of attacks at Phuoc Vinh had subsided substantially, and the few rounds that did come our way seemed to always be aimed at the 9th Cavalry or the 20th Aerial Rocket Artillery flight lines. Apparently they did not like Cobra helicopters. It was obvious that the enemy respected and feared the retaliation of the new powerful tenant at Phuoc Vinh.

The change of command, making me Tide 6, would not occur for about three weeks, giving me time to get acquainted with some of the key people I would soon be working with as well as flying time to get reacquainted with the CH-47. I would get my flight training from the Longhorns and the Wildcats, both located at Bearcat, just south of Ben Hoa. This gave me a chance to spend some time with both commanders, Major George Kieffer of A Company, and Major Ed Hogan of B Company. I flew primarily with CWO Paul Getz, an instructor pilot at A Company, the Wildcats.

I soon learned that the 1st Air Cavalry's employment of CH-47 Chinooks didn't deviate much from how we used them in the 1st Aviation Brigade. My assigned unit, Charlie company, was the only company in the 228th equipped with the B model Chinooks. The difference was that the A model had a payload of ten thousand pounds, and the B model could up that another five thousand pounds. Pathfinders and riggers were instructed to limit loads to eight thousand pounds for CH-47A aircraft. The B model also had a cruise speed of 150 knots compared to 130 knots for the A model. I quickly learned that the added lift capacity carried with it some pride as Crimson Tide aircraft often volunteered to help the other companies after their sorties had been completed. I also noted that the carrying of double external loads was common practice with Crimson Tide aircraft.

In addition to honing my piloting skills in the CH-47, I had enough time to become acquainted with the people I felt I would be interacting with most. My recent Ft. Stewart command experience convinced me I had better pay a visit to the JAG office and introduce myself. Surely they would be seeing a lot of me in the near future. Fortunately, this proved to be a major waste of time as I never even administered an Article 15 during my tenure as company commander of Charley company. I was to soon find out what good non-commissioned officers can do for the morale and discipline of a unit. Of course, being busy and engaged in war also helps to keep people from getting too mischievous.

I also knew, as every aviation commander knows, that success or failure as an aviation commander depends on availability of aircraft to perform the mission. My forte as a Chinook commander favored the operational aspects of the job. I was not strong in the maintenance area and would rely heavily on people that were. My immediate concern would center on the near term DEROS of the company maintenance officer, Captain George Moore. I remembered what my new commanding officer had told me about five minutes after our introduction: "Your mission is to make sure you provide six flyable birds, seven days a week." That pronouncement was almost immediately followed with the disconcerting news that I would soon be losing my maintenance officer, who, I was told, was superb. *Great!* I thought to myself.

On the surface, providing six flyable daily does not appear that challenging, particularly with an assignment of sixteen aircraft, but anyone who has ever been around Chinooks knows better. The Chinook is a maintenance monster that requires a 7/24 effort. Charley company had a maintenance detachment of about one hundred additional men over and above the TOE of the Assault Support Helicopter Company's complement of maintenance personnel. This augmentation allowed for the scheduling of two daily twelve hour shifts that were needed to keep those pack of six (six pack) airborne. I spent a lot of time on the flight line and observed that we had some real talented and devoted people there. The Boeing Vertol Tech Rep, Mr. Glenn Miller, was impressive, dedicated, and involved in every aspect of maintenance activity. CWO Gary Parsons, Captain Moore's assistant was likewise impressive, but it was readily apparent that the strong leadership of Captain Moore would be sorely missed. The maintenance crew was accomplishing its mission at present, but what would be the effect of losing Captain Moore, and who would replace him?

The aviators I was meeting in Charley company were certainly younger than the 213th CH-47 pilots I had flown with during my last tour. Youth has its advantages and disadvantages. The obvious disadvantage would be lack of experience. Every aviator experiences a lot of cheap mistakes during the elementary years of flying. Experience in aviation, like everything else, is the ultimate teacher. One hopes that the cheap lessons learned early are not punctuated with expensive ones, but generally the punctuation tends to be sloppier in the early years of flying. On the brighter side, however, was the enthusiasm and professionalism I was observing. To my surprise a couple of the WO1s, affectionately called "Wobbly Ones," had even been designated aircraft commanders. I would also soon find out that the prevalence of the Catch 22 syndrome that I had observed occasionally in the 213th bordered on the nonexistent. I was becoming excited; these guys were Crimson Tide, but they were going to be my Fighting Illini.

My worries about replacing the coming maintenance officer vacancy would be allayed before Captain Moore's DEROS. An Infantry officer, Captain John Smith, would approach me and ask for the job. His request was done so with such confidence and sincerity that I agreed to give him a go at it. And go he did. Within four months of my taking command, the Crimson Tide would be averaging almost fourteen hundred flying hours per month, exceeding the USARV average for CH-47 companies by a full 50 percent. In spite of the unusually high flying hours attained, Captain Smith and his maintenance team were able to maintain an aircraft availability in excess of 80 percent. This represented an availability that was 15 percent above the DA goal of CH-47 helicopter availability. During the Cambodian Incursion a couple of months later, the Crimson Tide would exceed all previous monthly flight records for medium lift helicopter units when it flew 1770 hours in a single month and still it maintained 80 percent aircraft availability. Saying "Go for it," to Captain Smith when he ask for the maintenance officer job was the best decision I made during the entire time I commanded the Crimson Tide. Ironically, it was my very first decision and was made even before I took command of the company.

The other great gift I had was the First Sergeant who came with company. His name was Robert M. Bratton, and I soon became convinced that there was no better First Sergeant in the U.S. Army. He was impressive and tough looking, lean, and trim. I would find out just how tough he was after I got closer to him. I learned that he had fought for the Salt Lake City Golden Gloves Middleweight Championship and won the championship belt. He never pursued boxing after he won the championship but instead chose to enlist and make the Army his profession. His opponent in the championship bout, Gene Fulmer, elected to make boxing his profession and later became the Middleweight Champion of the World. He ran a tight company, and that's why I didn't have to go through what I had experienced at Ft. Stewart. First Sergeant Bratton was my JA. He was from the old school and was not opposed to taking somebody behind the shed if it was warranted. Nobody cared to take that trip with him. But being a tough First Sergeant is just half the story about First Sergeant Bratton. We would be selected as the company in the battalion to be inspected by the USARV Inspector General. Administratively he scored almost a perfect score, yet he was mad at himself for a couple of minor administrative shortcomings that were noted on the final report.

1st Sergeant Bratton...One Tough Top!

A Cloud Over My
Change of Command

When you are in a war zone, holidays and special festive days like Halloween seem to slip by, but I will forever remember the Halloween of 1969 for two reasons. First it was day that I would take command of Charley Company. The ceremony was hardly a gala affair. The guidon was passed to me, I signed for all the property, and that was it. The second reason was the shocking news that arrived right after I officially became Tide 6. The operations NCO, Sergeant Krebs, came into the orderly room and announced that he had just gotten news that CWO Paul Getz of A Company was killed in a helicopter accident near his home base of Bearcat. We learned later that his Chinook had had the only known dual hydraulic failure. Reportedly, Paul was communicating in a jovial manner with his home base operations, reporting that he was getting a shower of hydraulic fluid as it was running down his neck. He was flying just off the deck when both hydraulic systems failed. He pancaked the aircraft and it slid with its forward momentum across an open field, but the nose of the aircraft dipped into a ravine and Paul's side of the cockpit crashed into a stump, crushing him. He was the only fatality among the crew of five, and the others suffered no serious injuries.

I had met Paul during my previous tour and so was familiar with his reputation for being a real fine aviator and professional officer. I really got to know and respect him during the recent check out he had given me and through the flying hours we had shared just a couple of weeks earlier. He was liked and respected by everyone, up and down the line. It would be a huge blow to the morale of the Wildcats.

The Crimson Tide had recently had its own run of bad luck. On September 3, 1969, Captain Larry Mohler, the company IP, and his co-pilot, CW3 Dean Lange, landed in a supposedly secured ARVN LZ. While on the ground and at flight idle, an enemy soldier appeared only a few yards directly in front of them and fired a RPG

106

round through the pilot's windshield. The round hit Mr. Lange in the head, killing him instantly, passed through the firewall between the cockpit and the fuselage, and exited out the rear of the helicopter before detonating. This series of pictures is Mohler and Lang's aircraft, Crimson Tide 6718473. Note in photo 1 where the RPG projectile passed through left windshield and fire wall behind removed pilots seat. Photo 2 shows a close up where the projectile went through the fire wall. Photo 3 shows a stripped aircraft 6718473, ready for airlift to 15th Transportation Corps Battalion for repair. Photo 4 is 6718473's ride to depot repair.

Photo 1

Photo 2

Photo 3

Photo 4

On September 30, 1969, SFC Overacker was killed by a mortar shrapnel while standing in the pay line in the company area. Then, just ten days later, a Crimson Tide crewman, Flight Engineer, SP5 Walter Bartasch, was killed by a 12.7 mm anti-aircraft ground fire while his aircraft was in flight working in the AO. I knew none of the men killed but was in the company area soon after and during all these combat losses and noticed the demoralizing impact on the company.

I had heard about Captain Mohler's ordeal during my initial meeting with my predecessor and my thought was, what kind of impact would that have on one's ability to function as the unit's instructor pilot? After coming back to Phuoc Vinh from my flight training with the Wildcats and Longhorns, I was scheduled to fly missions with the Crimson Tide. I was eager to tryout the more powerful CH-47B model. I was also pleased that I was scheduled to fly with our unit IP, Captain Mohler, since I was interested in how he was handling his horrendous experience after about five weeks. I found him cool and competent. He was a fine pilot and extremely knowledgeable of the aircraft's systems and capabilities. He would remain our company IP, that was for sure.

Crimson Tide 6

I may have been troubled with the unit call sign, but nobody else was. And why should they be? University of Alabama football teams had eight National Championships to their credit, the most recent being in 1961, 1964, and 1965 under Coach Paul "Bear" Bryant. I admired Coach Bryant, not so much for his national titles, but more for his credo with respect to what he looked for in a football player. He was quoted as saying, "What matters is not the size of the dog in the fight, but the size of the fight in the dog." Being an undersized lineman, that was my kind of philosophy. If I couldn't be Tomahawk 6, being Tide 6 wasn't all that bad, and it certainly was preferable over the call signs of the other two Chinook units in the battalion.

I decided early on that since I was announcing to the world over FM and UHF radio waves that I was head coach of the Crimson Tide in Vietnam, I might just as well communicate with the head coach of the Crimson Tide back in Tuscaloosa, Alabama. So, with the help of the First Sergeant and Captain Rick Storm, we sat down and collectively drafted a letter for Coach Bryant to inform him that there was, indeed, another Crimson Tide team on this planet. We told him we were proud of our name and that he and his team would likewise be proud of our achievements. The letter included some details about what we did for a living and how we went about doing it. We also included a company guidon flag and a couple of action photographs of our aircraft supporting 1st Cavalry soldiers in the field. About a month later we received a letter from Coach Bryant and a Crimson Tide football. One panel of the football was signed by Coach Bryant, his football coaching staff, and the entire 1969 football squad. Because of Coach Bryant's popularity, Charley Company gained a little notoriety, as his gesture was written up in the Stars and Stripes newspaper together with the picture shown on the following page.

The Crimson Tide photo taken on January 8, 1970, at Camp Gorvad, Phuoc Vinh, in front of the C/228th Chinook revetments. This is obviously not the SEC Crimson Tide; this is the Southeast Asia Crimson Tide! The SEA linemen from left end to right end are: CW2 Gary Parsons, CPT John Smith, CPT Larry Mohler, 1LT Jim Lemaster, CW1 Larry Covey, CPT George Moore, and CW2 Steve Lindholm. In the backfield, from left to right are: CW2 John Moore, CW2 Rick Wilken, Major Bob Lanzotti, CPT Harrold Merrick, 1LT Rick Storm, and CW2 Davis.

When I left the unit, about seven months later, the officers and men of Charlie Company signed the remaining two panels of the ball and gave it to me as a going away gift. Today that ball resides in my home as one of my most prized possessions.

Ironically, the last of Coach Bryant's twenty-four straight bowl appearances would be against the Fighting Illini in the Liberty Bowl on December 29, 1982. It was Coach Bryant's last game, and its outcome would advance his win column from 322 to 323. While my loyalty remained with the Fighting Illini during the entire game, the disappointment of the final score was certainly diminished by my affiliation with the Crimson Tide of Vietnam. Like the rest of the football world, and certainly all the Vietnam Crimson Tide, I was pleased that Coach Bryant improved his winning percentage in the very last game he would coach. Hell, I just wish his last game hadn't been against the Illini. I grew to love that call sign, Crimson Tide 6. Everyone loves a winner.

The Hook

This is a book of stories, and "The Hook," wouldn't you agree, is a great title for a story. But the following isn't exactly a story; actually, it is an introduction to one of the main players of this book. It introduces and familiarizes you with the CH-47 Chinook, the aircraft you've already read some about, but more is on the way. Virtually every story from here to the end will involve the Chinook in some manner. Since a picture is worth a thousand words, the narrative will be short and the pictures are many. The Chinook's nickname is the Hook or Shithook. I prefer calling it the Hook, because I rather like the old bird. As military aircraft go, it has attained senior status as it has been the primary Army medium lift helicopter for over forty continuous years. During my two tours in Vietnam, there were three models introduced to the Army. The CH-47A was delivered to the Army during 1962. It was the Chinook model I was qualified in and the aircraft I flew during my first tour in Vietnam. The CH-47B was introduced and delivered to the Army during 1967. It increased the payload from ten thousand to fifteen thousand pounds and offered greater stability and airspeed. The CH-47B was the aircraft I flew during my second tour in Vietnam. The CH-47C model was delivered to the Army during late 1968. Its improvement offered a substantial increase of payload capability as well as a minor bump in airspeed. I never flew the CH-47C, but if I ever used the term Shithook, it would probably be directed to this model (See story, "CH-47C minus CH-47B equals Zero" in this tour). The CH-47C was the mainstay until 1980 when the CH-47D was introduced. Today we're all the way up to the CH-47E model. I don't know what that thing will lift or do, but for $32-plus million, they ought to do a lot more than what I flew more than three decades ago.

The primary mission of the Hook in Vietnam was to air transport artillery pieces and ammunition. The cornerstone of conducting successful airmobility operations is based on Nathan Bedford Forrest's Civil War battle plan of "Getting there firstest with the mostest." Lift ships put the infantry on the enemy and the Hooks give the Infantry artillery fire support. The Hook can place artillery in terrain heretofore inaccessible during past conflicts. Fighting and pursuing enemy in a jungle environment would appreciably compound Infantry operations without the immediate availability of direct fire support. The following photographs show the way Hooks move artillery together with ammunition. The first photograph shows the hook landing a howitzer with its piggy back. More often than not, the gun crew would already be on the ground ready to receive their howitzer and put it into operation as quickly as possible. The pilot first sets the ammunition down, then moves the howitzer slightly forward to avoid sitting it down on the ammunition. This operation is orchestrated over the aircraft intercom by either the crew chief or flight engineer, who has positioned himself over the opening above the hook. The pilot becomes quite adept at landing piggy back loads after it has been performed over and over. Movement of Artillery was almost a daily event and was referred to as Fire Support Base (FSB) moves.

Notice the amount of dust caused by the rotor wash in the second photograph. Hook rotor blades generate one hundred mile per hour winds and stir up dust and debris galore. Recipients had a love-hate relationship with the Hook. It brought beans and bullets, but also hurricane winds.

Hooks and Howitzers: Have gun will travel!

The photograph below shows a hasty fire support base or temporary artillery encampment. Artillerymen may spend only a couple of days at this site, then move by Hook to another location to optimize fire support of forward ground operations. FSB moves, once underway could be completed within minutes and with as few as thirty Hook sorties.

The cockpit seats two pilots, dual controls and instrument panels. The radios are located in the center panel between the pilots. The aircraft commander generally sits in the left seat and his co-pilot in the right seat. The Chinook is one of the most stable helicopters I have ever flown. The seats are comfortable and the visibility is excellent. Its stability in flight makes it an outstanding aircraft for instrument flying in inclement weather.

CH-47 cockpit

The following series of pictures show Red hat riggers hooking up a variety of cargo for aerial lift to forward bases. The final two pictures show the flight engineer (or crew chief) looking through cargo hold where Hook is located. If you look closely you will see smoke on the ground beneath the howitzer. Colored smoke was popped by the recipient, then identified and confirmed by the pilot. The smoke marks the spot where the howitzer is wanted.

Hooking a Howitzer

Moving artillery ammo to fire support bases.

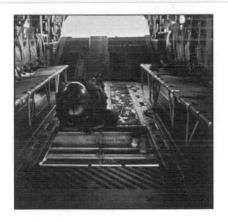

Crew chief communicating with the pilot as the artillery piece is lowered to the ground.

Chinooks can carry troops too. The book calls for thirty-three combat equipped troops, but I've personally packed as many as ninety ARVN on one single sortie.

The prime air assault mover for troops in Vietnam was the UH-1, Huey. The Chinook's primary mission was to move beans, bullets, artillery pieces, water and fuel in blivets, and anything and everything the troops needed in the AO, provided it weighed under 8 tons.

The Dudley Do-right Award

I never got a decent haircut from a Vietnamese barber. They used those hand clippers that looked more suited for cutting grass. I did, however, get a good idea from the Phouc Vinh barbershop that serviced our unit, and it may have paid dividends during my tour and maybe even after, who knows. Our barber had a concession in his shop and sold uniform paraphernalia such as unit emblems, badges, epaulets, patches, plaques, and that kind of thing. One metal badge caught my attention and triggered the idea. It was a depiction of a soldier with his head up his ass. For the life of me, I cannot recall how it looked now, but there was no mistake about its characterization. It was definitely a soldier with his head up his ass.

I got the idea that what if we, as a part of our safety program, discussed once a week the dumbest thing we did or saw being done while flying our aircraft, then perhaps we could learn from someone else's cheap mistake. The winner, the person who had the biggest bone headed deed, would be presented the badge with the guy's head up his ass, which he would be required to wear until the next meeting, one week hence. I bought the badge and discussed my idea with our company's Safety Officer. We agreed that we would surface the idea at our next safety meeting. We dubbed the badge the Dudley Do-right Award.

The safety officer presented the idea by explaining that the confessionals were not meant to belittle or demean but to simply avoid repeating mistakes that could result in a serious aircraft incident or accident. Everyone liked the idea and agreed to adopt it and begin holding an open court once a week. What followed was amazing. Some of the testimonials were downright unbelievable, most were hilarious, and virtually all were scary and potentially catastrophic. Opportunity abounds to make judgmental or thoughtless errors during a twelve hour flying day under perilous conditions. Many were caught and reported.

Catching the unit instructor pilot or aircraft commanders committing a flying *faux pas* deserving of the Dudley Do-right Award delighted all. But then, seeing the same guy wearing the award in consecutive weeks, or as the habitual recipient, tended to make aircraft commanders a wee bit wary when that person's name appeared adjacent to their name on the next day's mission schedule. I would hope that our Dudley Do-right program influenced the reduction of incidents and accidents, but the prevalence of blunders persisted throughout my tour with Charley Company.

Winged Warrior 6

During the Vietnam War, command time in company to brigade size units was limited to about six months for officers. When I assumed command of the Crimson Tide, my immediate boss, Winged Warrior 6, Lieutenant Colonel Bush, was working his final innings as the commander of the 228th ASH battalion. His replacement would be a Transportation Corps officer by the name of Lieutenant Colonel Francis J. Toner. Since my command tour would be extended a couple of months beyond the standard six months, he would remain my boss throughout my command of Charlie Company. Unlike the other two companies located at Bearcat, the proximity of my orderly room to his battalion headquarters was less than the length of a football field. I suppose the nearness promoted the closeness that developed between Lieutenant Colonel Toner and myself, but as everyone who has ever met him will attest, he was an easy man to admire and like. I could not have had a better mentor during a period that should prove to be the most challenging of my Army career, and my life for that matter.

During one of our initial meetings, Lieutenant Colonel Toner asked me outright, "What can I do to help you accomplish your mission?" Undoubtedly, he asked the other two company commanders the same question. My response, without hesitation, was, "Come and fly with us occasionally!" My suggestion was not made in a presumptuous manner. I was convinced, from previous tour's experience, that S-3s and commanders need to be where their people are rendering combat support to ground units. I believed that the involvement of S-3s and commanders had an inspirational impact on pilots. Colonel Soucek, the 11th Group commander and Lieutenant Colonel Toner's boss, was clearly a strong believer in the same conviction; he was constantly flying in the AO, monitoring the mission support of his three battalions. Either Lieutenant Colonel Toner concurred in my suggestion or he

Winged Warrior 6, LTC Frank Toner

had the same notion, because for the remainder of his tour as commander of the 228th, he would fly with each of his three companies about once a week.

These were not one and two hour ash and trash milk runs. His daily commitment began at o'dark-thirty in the morning when he pitched in and pre-flighted the aircraft and ended when the last sortie was completed at days end, usually long after the sun went down. Then he routinely wrote letters of commendation to compliment deserving crew members. During those days when he did not fly with his companies, he was usually airborne or about to be airborne in his Winged Warrior UH-1D. If there was an accident or combat related incident involving injury or fatality, Winged Warrior 6 would be one of the first on the scene. He soon became everyone's epitome of a commander. The officers and men of the 228th were not the only ones to recognize that they had a crown jewel in charge. When Lieutenant Colonel Toner finished his six months tour as Winged Warrior 6 and head coach of the Wildcats, Longhorns, and Crimson Tide, he would assume command of another 1st Cavalry Division battalion, the 15th Transportation Corps Battalion (Aircraft Maintenance and Supply).

Commanding successive units in one, 12 month overseas tour was virtually unheard of, but Toner had that kind of talent and the tenacity to "just do it," long before that phrase was ever even thought of. Frank Toner would rise eventually to stardom. He would be promoted to major general, then tragically would retire from the Army after discovery of pancreatic cancer, and would later succumb to the disease on February 14, 1988. For all who knew and flew with him, I am sure we would to the man agree that if call signs are passed out in heaven, "Winged Warrior 6" is taken.

Close Camaraderie of the Third Kind

While the pilots flew all the aircraft, flight engineers, crew chiefs, and gunners worked on assigned aircraft as teams. There were exceptions, particularly with gunners. A gunner was generally an Infantry 11 Bravo (Rifleman) who came from one of the Division's Infantry or Cavalry field units. One gunner, Private Doolittle, would not fly with anybody except CW3 Harry Stevens, a New Englander and a particularly popular officer among the enlisted flight crews. Whenever Harry went up, Doolittle went with — no questions, no arguments were ever attempted. That's just the way it was. You would have thought Private Doolittle was Harry's aide-de-camp as he was constantly in the presence of Harry. The gunner on a Chinook mans a M60, 7.62 mm machine gun on a swivel and is stationed on the left side of the fuselage, directly behind aircraft commander's seat. A fire wall separated the two. The aircraft commander and co-pilot changed FM frequencies constantly and UHF frequencies less frequently, but there was always on board intercom between crew members.

On one mission CW3 Stevens and his crew were flying in supplies for a non-divisional unit, a 11th Armored Cavalry Regiment (11ACR) which was attached to the 1st Cavalry Division and assigned a screening and reconnaissance role. The season was dry, and landings in a Chinook could sometimes be hazardous because of blowing dust and debris from the rotor wash. Harry made his approach into one of the few areas where he could release his sling load of ammo and supplies. He also had some internal cargo and needed to land from a hover.

During this process Harry's aircraft was creating a huge dust storm, and that didn't set too well with one 11th ACR trooper who had been sunning himself on top of an Armored Personnel Carrier (APC). While the cargo was being off-loaded, this enraged guy went berserk. He jumped off his APC and ran toward the Chinook. He then attempted to punch Harry through the cockpit window and had to literally jump off the ground to deliver his blows to his target, Harry's head, which was a good seven or eight feet off the ground. The blows, even if they found their mark, could not have inflicted pain as Harry was wearing his flight helmet, which was every bit as protective as a football helmet. Harry had just transmitted over the intercom something to the effect of, "Look at this crazy SOB!" Private Doolittle, with his gun trained on the deranged soldier, transmitted over the intercom to his aircraft commander, "Sir, do you want me to blow his shit away?" Harry's immediate reply was, "No, don't shoot!" There could be no doubt that if Harry's command had been to the affirmative, there would surely be one more name inscribed on the Vietnam Memorial today.

Pay Back is Hell

On January 20, 1970, CWO Steve Lindholm and his co-pilot, Captain Bill Norton, were on a routine resupply mission carrying a sling load of several five hundred - gallon rubber water blivets. They were flying at an altitude of about three thousand feet over the Iron Triangle, near Lai Khe, right in the middle of War Zone C. Steve, like myself, had experienced 51 caliber and 12.7mm anti-aircraft tracers coming his way at night. The tracers do, in fact, look like orange basketballs being thrown in your direction. On this clear day, Steve would catch a glimpse of fast moving red flecks streaking skyward to his front right. Moments later, and coincidentally with seeing his master caution panel light up like a Christmas tree, the flight engineer transmitted over the intercom, "Sir, we've got a fire back here!" Oil pressure fell in the right engine and the fire warning light came on. Steve pulled the T-handle, shut down the right engine, and transmitted his mayday over UHF, then lowered his thrust control, initiating a forced landing.

The volume of Army and Air Force air traffic in War Zone C was undoubtedly the most heavily concentrated in all of South Vietnam. When Steve transmitted his mayday, there was more than enough response and assistance available. Steve's first respondent was an USAF Forward Air Controller (FAC) in close proximity. With Steve's help the FAC actually spotted Crimson Tide 6718487 as it was going down. The FAC also spotted tracers from the enemy gun, still concentrating its fire on the aircraft they just hit. The FAC now had the gun's location pinpointed and reported target coordinates to his TAC. Steve or Bill had transmitted a situation report to the Crimson Tide operations center. Help was on the way.

While auto-rotating down to a clearing selected as the landing site, Steve was communicating alternately with the FAC and his flight engineer to determine the extent and status of the fire. He learned that the fire appeared to be only on the right side of the aircraft and was concentrated in the vicinity of the right engine pod. The flight engineer reported that he had the fire extinguisher bottle in hand and was going to lower the ramp to gain better access to the fire. When he lowered the ramp, the fire rushed into the rear fuselage and singed all the exposed hair on both the flight engineer and crew chief. The ramp was quickly closed, and there was no further attempt to put out the fire while the aircraft was airborne. Steve completed the auto-rotative landing successfully without further damage to the aircraft. When the aircraft touched down, crew members used fire extinguishers to smother the fire.

The FAC had not only requested his own strike on the enemy gun but was now communicating with cobra gunships circling over Crimson Tide 487 and directing them to the gun emplacement about one mile from 487. Steve still had radio communication with our Crimson Tide operations, who was assuring him that help was on the way in the form of guns and slicks from the 1st Squadron, 9th Cavalry. While Steve was working the radio in the cockpit, he suddenly realized the absence of his co-pilot, Captain Norton. He called out for him several times before getting a response that sounded as if it came well forward of the aircraft. The Standard Operating Procedures (SOP) for down Chinooks designates specific stations for crew members to establish a perimeter defense. Obviously Bill, an Academy graduate, had delved into the SOP. He was correctly stationed directly in front of the aircraft, pistol drawn, pointed toward the tree line, and ready for action.

The enemy gunner may have ruined Steve and Bill's day, but two Cobra gunships and two F4 Phantoms provided some serious payback. The 1st of the 9th Cavalrymen were inserted near the gun emplacement. They advanced without opposition and recovered the weapon. The enemy was using a captured U.S. 50 caliber machine gun, now recaptured. Later Winged Warrior 6, who was at the scene of downed aircraft, was presented the weapon, or rather the remains of the weapon. The gun that downed Crimson Tide 487 would not make a good war trophy as it, like its gunner, had not fared well after 500 bound bombs and salvos of 2.75 in rockets.

Crimson Tide 6818487 had considerable fire damage on its right aft pylon and engine section. After thorough inspection to determine airworthiness, it was determined that 487 could be flown home with one engine. Captain Larry Mohler, the company IP, and Captain Smith, the maintenance officer, picked the aircraft up to a hover and continued to hover for several minutes before taking off. The flight back to Phouc Vinh was made without further incident. For Steve's skill in saving the crew and aircraft, together with directing and helping the FAC locate the enemy, he was awarded the Distinguished Flying Cross.

Back in the Crimson Tide maintenance area it was finally determined that 6718487 had too much fire damage to be repaired in-country. It was decided that the airframe would DEROS to the U.S. Army Depot, New Cumberland, Pennsylvania. Ironically the 6718487 would burn again, this time totally. A USAF C-133, with Crimson Tide 6718487 aboard, crashed and burned five miles northeast of Palisade, Nebraska, on February 6, 1970. This would be the first of five Crimson Tide aircraft to be destroyed in the next five months.

The first of the following two photographs shows Crimson Tide 6718487 back at Phuoc Vinh where it was being cannibalized for parts before its journey to New Cumberland, Pennsylvania. The second shows 6718487 departing Phuoc Vinh by CH-54 airlift to Tan San Nhut Airport at Saigon where it would be loaded into the ill-fated USAF C-133.

The extent of exterior fire damage.
The engine was completely destroyed.

Sayonara, Crimson Tide 6718487!

Soaring Systolic Story

Will Rogers said, "I've never met a man I didn't like." Unfortunately I have met a few. Among the few was a 1st Air Cav flight surgeon stationed at Phuoc Vinh. I am sure the feeling was mutual. I think it was just a personality misfit right from the get go. I thought he was a smart ass and got the impression that he thought I was a dumb ass. Our meetings always seemed to transmit our mutual thoughts and feelings loud and clear.

During the period when Crimson Tide pilots were flying in the two-hundred hour per month range, the good flight surgeon made it a practice to walk into our club every evening around 2000 hours and check each and every pilot's blood pressure. This was the method he used to determine if the pilots were fit to fly the next day. I didn't question the procedure, but it was a wee bit irksome when tomorrow's schedule was already prepared and had to be completely revised. As stated earlier, I did not have as many Catch 22 syndrome cases as I had seen during my last tour, but we had a couple. It irritated me when I saw him scratch those names, because they sure looked fit to me.

This story doesn't have so much to do with that problem as it does with a personal story that I thought humorous enough to mention, so here goes. The good flight surgeon made it a practice to always check my blood pressure first on his nightly visit. I don't know why. Perhaps he just wanted to get it out of the way. Often he would comment and compliment me about my good blood pressure range. What did he expect, I was only thirty-three years old!

One evening we had just completed showing a porno movie obtained by one of the pilots during his recent R&R somewhere. In fact I think someone had just made a suggestion to rewind and replay it, when in came the flight surgeon. He walked right over to me as usual, and I extended my arm for the blood pressure cuff. He always used his stethoscope while taking the reading. I was watching his eyes get big as he undoubtedly became dumbfounded with my sky-high systolic blood pressure. He said, "Jesus, what happened to you?" I explained what I thought had just happened to me. Obviously we had thrown him a curve ball. The thing is, I thought it funny, he thought it irritating. But he put us in extra innings by stating that he would come back later. No doubt to screw up our lineup once again. Smart-ass doctor!

The above picture is BG Shoemaker presenting our unit with a plaque on February 8, 1970, to recognize an achievement of flying five thousand CH-47 hours without an accident. Exactly thirty-one days later our unit would experience a catastrophic accident that we would have traded all the plaques and awards in the world to undo. As accidents go in aviation, "Fate is the hunter," and fate would find us on March 9, 1970, and a couple of more times as well.

The Accident

Two-thirds of the Chinook assets In the 1st Air Cavalry Division were CH-47A models. Since the maximum payload of a CH-47A is ten thousand pounds, the quartermaster riggers at staging sites prepared sling loads in the eight thousand pound range. The remaining one-third of the division medium lift helicopter assets belonged to the Crimson Tide. We were flying the newer CH-47B model that bumped the payload to fifteen thousand pounds. As stated earlier, the Crimson Tide often assisted its sister units in the AO, simply because the CH-47B was faster, could lift more, and was generally finished with its sorties earlier than the Wildcats and Longhorns. It was also common practice to see the Crimson Tide aircraft picking up double sling loads, particularly when fire support base moves were being executed and time was of the essence.

It doesn't take much of a mathematician to figure out that two eight thousand pound loads will exceed the published payload capacity of a CH-47B. We had a few math lessons during our safety meetings as hauling double loads was a much talked about topic and one of my major flight safety concerns. Did Crimson Tide aircraft commanders sometimes exceed the published payload limit? The answer to that question would be yes, they probably did. Personally I have hauled double loads many times. It wasn't risky business if one used common sense. For example did each of the loads actually weigh eight thousand pounds? Could the ground riggers arrange double loads that were compatible with the payload capability of the CH-47B? What was the status of the fuel on board? After all, the B model's fuel capacity was one thousand gallons of JP4 at six and one-half pounds per gallon. The hover check while picking up the load was probably the single most deciding factor. To be honest, I have about eight hundred hours of transporting sling loads in the CH-47B, and I can't recall ever having to sit a single or a double load down.

On March 9, 1970, Crimson Tide 6619106 was working in the Binh Long Province and flying resupply sorties out of Quan Loi Airfield to various Fire Support Bases in the vicinity of Song Be. The aircraft commander, CWO John Fortner, and his co-pilot, CWO Terry Anderson, were hovering over a heavy load of engineer materiel (concertina wire) used for constructing a perimeter defense around LZs and FSBs. The barbed wire was picked up, then Crimson Tide 106 hovered over a second heavy load of engineer materiel, this time three bundles each of three and eight foot steel stakes. CWO Steve Lindholm was airborne in another Crimson Tide aircraft in the Quan Loi airfield traffic pattern and watched Crimson Tide 106 picking up the second sling load at the PZ helipad. The hookup was made; 106 hovered over the load momentarily, but lowered it to the ground, released it, and backed off for another try. The aircraft commander would then allow his confidence in the aircraft's capability as well as his own flying skills override prudent judgment. Tragically it would be a fatal mistake.

CWO Lindholm watched 106 hover back over the double load, pick it up to a low hover, and slowly began moving forward to gain sufficient airspeed to achieve translational lift. After the accident, riggers and other personnel at the staging site, who heard CH-47 aircraft continuously throughout the day, said that they had never heard a Chinook make the sounds that Crimson Tide 106 was making during its horrific flight. What they heard was a combination of bleed band popping around the engines' compressors and the noise of coning tandem rotor blades as their RPM dropped dangerously toward the minimum requisite for flight. In the cockpit the crew of Crimson Tide 6619106 was experiencing more than low rotor RPM. They were also dragging a load on the runway that they could not release. Several witnesses on the ground at Quan Loi stated that they heard gunfire coming from the underside of 106. Some surmised that the flight crew was trying to shoot and sever the nylon donut ring suspending the sling load to the hook. The recovered sling gear did show evidence of what appeared to be bullet damage.

While dragging the load, the nose of the aircraft tucked forward and the rotors appeared to almost strike the ground. Some of the engineer stakes were spewing on the runway as the aircraft floundered to gain altitude. As the aircraft finally started to slowly ascend, the sling load began swinging fore and aft and the aircraft began to porpoise with the load's instability. When the aircraft reached an altitude of about five hundred feet, the remainder of the load finally released. The load hit and destroyed an unoccupied UH-1H parked in its revetment. When the load released, 106 ascended, rolled on its left side, then inverted. One of the aft rotors slammed into the aircraft's fuselage, and the aircraft broke up into three major pieces. Only the aft pylon section burned. WO1 John L. Fortner, WO1 Terrance W. Anderson, Flight Engineer SP4 Keith H. Reitz, Crew Chief SP4 George A. Bamford, and Door Gunner Phillip L. Clark, all found in the forward section, were killed instantly upon impact.

The site and sounds of that crash will forever be in the memory of Steve Lindholm, who not only witnessed the crash but heard the pilots over the radio during their fateful attempt to get control of the aircraft. I heard about the crash within minutes of its occurrence. Within a couple of hours after the accident, I was at Quan Loi Airfield and had found the quartermaster graves registration officer, who had already recovered the bodies from the aircraft. He gave me their dog tags and I was following him to where the bodies were assembled. He said to me, "Major, they are dead and its not necessary for you to see them." I said, "Okay, thank you." I really did not want to see them, and to this day I am thankful that the quartermaster officer gave me an option.

Losing friends and comrades in battle is tough and demoralizing, but it can be explained. It can be understood. Losing them in an accident, when an aircraft comes apart, involves all those intangibles that created fear and diffidence, particularly among pilots and crew members who knew and flew with those who died in 106. The accident and loss of the crew were devastating to the morale of the Crimson Tide. While I had a lot of letters to write, I thought my best contribution to the company was to climb into one of those Crimson Tide aircraft on March 10, 1970 and fly in it all day long. The crash of 106 was the most traumatic experience of my tour.

I have a wonderful post script to this tragic event. It started just a few weeks before the accident. CWO John Fortner requested permission to go on a R&R to Hawaii to take care of some personal business. I was led to believe that his personal business would have to be conducted in his home state. I approved his request, and within a month after his return he was killed. Then, a month or so after the accident, I learned that his wife was pregnant. At that time I remember thinking that I wished I had not granted him permission to go on that R&R. Twenty-seven years later, members of the Crimson Tide gathered for their first reunion. The gala event was at the Space Needle restaurant in Seattle, on the Fourth of July, 1997. Seated directly across the table from me was John Fortner Jr. John Jr. was a clone of his father, in looks and all those other attributes that we all admired in his father. His mother had raised him as a single parent (she is now remarried) through his schooling years all the way through college. It was nice to think that my decision twenty-seven years earlier had contributed to something as extraordinary as this.

Cambodian Incursion

The TET Offensive of 1968 is commonly referred to as the turning point of the war. It inarguably evoked escalation on two fronts. It intensified the fighting in Vietnam, and it expanded the anti-war sentiment in the United States. Massive anit-war demonstrations were the order of the day on campuses throughout America. It is estimated that twenty-five million protested in our nation's capital during 1968 with the largest single day demonstration of two hundred and fifty thousand on November 15, 1968.

Public pressure influenced an announcement during mid-April 1970 to bring home within a year one hundred and fifty thousand of the one-half million troops already in South Vietnam. Then just days later, President Nixon addressed the nation and announced his decision to attack North Vietnamese and Viet Cong sanctuaries along the Cambodian border. The '68 TET Offensive may have gotten the anti-war ball rolling, but the Cambodian Incursion announced on January 30, 1970, by President Nixon really riled the protesters. Adding fuel to the fire, just four days after we crossed the borders and began destroying NVA and Viet Cong supply bases, the Ohio National Guard killed four college students at Kent State. It was the *coup de d'etat* that seemingly ended any hope of military victory in Vietnam. Its aftermath brought huge domestic opposition against continuation of the war.

During the fall of 1968, the 1st Air Cavalry Division moved from I Corps to III Corps, a distance of 350 miles. It's mission, besides "closing with and destroying the enemy," was to thwart another major TET Offensive. This would be accomplished by interdicting and sealing routes of infiltration coming into South Vietnam from Cambodia. The 3rd Brigade began moving the last week in October, 1968, followed by the 1st and 2nd Brigades during November. The entire division would conduct operations in four provinces, Phuoc

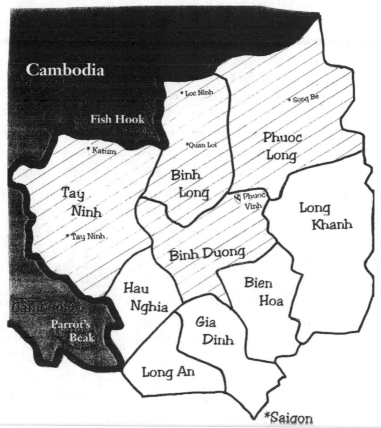

1st Air Cavalry Division's AO in III Corps

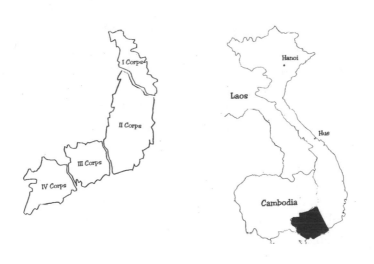

Long, Binh Long, Tay Ninh, and Bin Duong, an AO of about fourteen thousand square kilometers. Combat operations in its new AO quickly yielded considerable caches of weapons, ammunition, and food, but it was obvious that the major enemy supply bases were located in sanctuaries across the Cambodian border. The Parrot's Beak and Fish Hook regions along the border were the presumed harborers of these sanctuaries.

Vietnam was divided into four Corps, I Corps in the north and IV Corps in the south. During my tour with 1st Cavalry Division, the division operated solely in the III Corps area` and specifically in the provinces of Binh Long, Phuoc Long, Tay Ninh, and Binh Duong. The 1st Cavalry Division headquarters was located at Camp Gorvad, Phuoc Vinh. The map on the preceding page details the area of operations of the 1st Cavalry (Airmobile) Division.

We were, of course, well aware of the decaying support for our war effort in Vietnam. The *Stars and Stripes* was full of anit-war news that was definitely impacting on troop morale. Even the gung ho were beginning to doubt that their sacrifices and efforts were truly meaningful and important. On April 30, 1970, the Crimson Tide learned that President Nixon would be informing the American public that we would be conducting the Cambodian Incursion coincidentally with our crossing the borders into Cambodia. This news boosted our morale tremendously. Perhaps we really were in this war to win! The Crimson Tide's role in the attack would be to provide our usual six pack, and we were delighted to learn that we were selected to airlift the first artillery battery to be inserted into Cambodia. We learned that our crossing of the border would be prefaced by extensive B-52 and tactical air strikes, and one helluva artillery prep. Positioning of artillery to support our initial selected LZs in Cambodia did not give away our intentions to launch an attack because we were already operating extremely close to the borders, particularly in the Parrot's Beak and Fish Hook areas. Our 1st Air Cav modus operandi during the early spring of 1970 was to establish hasty fire bases for just a few days, then move them by Chinook. Hardly a day passed during the months of March through April that the Crimson Tide did not participate in a fire support base move. This was kickass air-mobile war.

The Cambodian campaign was a 7/24 operation, and Crimson Tide aircraft and crewmen were required to meet flight levels (tonnage and flying hours) never considered possible for a CH-47 unit. During the month of May of 1970, Charley Company exceeded 1,770 hours for the month. The success of the Cambodian Incursion also exceeded expectations. Two NVA supply bases, nicknamed The City and Rock Island East, had yielded some 2,600 weapons, over 10,000,000 rounds of ammunition, and more than 2,000 tons of rice. While large concentrations of enemy and the Central Office of South Vietnam (COSVN) headquarters were not found, the 1st Air Cav and units under its operational control (ARVN and 11th ACR) was credited with 2,574 enemy killed and 31 POWs taken. The sixty-day Incursion was considered one of the most successful operations in the history of the 1st Cavalry Division.

CH-47C minus CH-47B equals Zero

Naturally, everyone was apprehensive on the Cambodian Incursion D-day. In the end we were all happy to learn that the only thing we had to fear was fear itself. We had expected heavy machine gun fire at the minimum, and what we got was some small arm's fire that did not connect with any of our aircraft, although the initial assaulting slicks did get some hits. Command of the Cambodian Incursion was given to Brigadier General Shoemaker, the ADC of the 1st Air Cavalry. If General Shoemaker's plan included the element of surprise, I sure would like to buy the man a drink someday. The enemy obviously didn't have a clue. They, like the American public, were learning of the attack at the same time it was being conducted.

The Crimson Tide was not home free. Late in the evening, Crimson Tide 6619114, with CW2 Harry Stevens at the helm, was bringing in water to LZ East. Actually, Harry also had several cases of beer aboard which he had somehow obtained somewhere. Harry was...what every unit wants. Harry was...what our unit was lucky enough to have. Harry was...a scrounge. Harry knew how to deal and deal he did. Our company club was built entirely of teakwood, thanks to Harry's dealings with Special Forces somewhere, some way.

Harry was also one of the best pilots in the unit. On the morning of the push across the border, Harry's aircraft, 6619114, would be the first CH-47 aircraft to air-deliver a howitzer into Cambodia. It was not the first time Harry made it first to something. He had, just one year earlier, flown President Nixon's Secret Service to Vatican City for the President's historic visit with the Pope. He had piloted the first landing of a turbine powered helicopter in Vatican Square. Anyway, on this evening, Harry would land into a tight LZ, release his sling load, then land to off-load the beer. While moving to find a suitable landing surface, Crimson Tide 114 would clip some bamboo trees with its rotors. When Harry lifted to a hover, the aircraft vibrated so severely that he sat it back to the ground and shut down to inspect the rotor damage. The inspection revealed that the damage was more than expected, and the aircraft was correctly deemed unflyable.

Rotor replacement was out of the question because there was no way to get the type of equipment required to perform the rotor change into that restricted area. There was only one way to get Crimson Tide 6619114 out of LZ East. It would have to be by aerial recovery. The "Who you gonna call?" in this case would be none other than my old company, the 213th Black Cats, who had been recently equipped with the newer CH-47C. The "Super C" had a payload capacity of 23,000 pounds. The empty weight of a CH-47B model is 19,194 pounds. There was, of course, fuel on board Crimson Tide 114. The Black Cat CH-47C would have a maximum load.

The recovery would be performed the next morning, and CW2 Stevens and his crew would have to get some ground duty for the evening, as they would spend the night with their Infantry and Artillery brothers at LZ East. When I got back to the company that evening, First Sergeant Bratton informed me that CWO Stevens would be promoted from CW2 to CW3 effective May 1, 1970. Too bad he could not celebrate that evening, but I had a present all ready for CW2 (promotable) Stevens the following day. I departed early the following morning with Winged Warrior 6 in his UH-1H. We arrived about the same time as the Super C and orbited to watch the recovery team prepare Crimson Tide 114 for extraction. We made one low, slow pass over Crimson Tide 114, and I saw CW2 Stevens in its vicinity. I dropped a satchel containing three items: a letter of congratulations for being promoted to CW3, his official promotion orders, and probably most important for Harry and crew, several miniature bottles of Crown Royal whiskey.

Colonel Toner and I orbited until the hookup was made. We planned to pick up the Crimson Tide 114 crew on the ground, then follow the Super C back to Phuoc Vinh. The Super C lifted our aircraft to a hover, began its ascending takeoff, cleared the trees, then continued its climb to what appeared to be a successful recovery. We were about ready to make our approach into the LZ when I saw Crimson Tide 6619114 being air-mailed from about five hundred feet. I really don't know what happened. I'm not sure I even saw an after-action report on the failed recovery. I did know that we were minus one more aircraft, and that presented a foreboding dilemma as all of a sudden, we were down to thirteen aircraft.

Beer, Bravado, and BS

Our unit was never more than 75 percent strength in pilots. During the early months of my command of Charley company, pilots were flying, on the average, about 150 hours a month. This is a lot when one considers that FAA regulations limit commercial pilots to 100 hours per month and not more than 30 in a seven day period. Our flying hours would steadily go up to over 200 hours per month right before and during the Cambodian Incursion. I always rejoiced every time the First Sergeant informed me that we were getting a new pilot.

Unfortunately the newly arrived captain standing before me didn't have any more flight experience than a Wobbly 1, although he had been a platoon leader in a rifle company and appeared to have good leadership potential. About the time I was finishing up my briefing on the company, Captain Storm, who was going to give the new captain a company tour, joined us in the office. He informed me that the 1st of the 9th Cavalry was hosting a Ranger Reunion at their club that was located across the airfield at Phuoc Vinh. We were wearing cloth sewn subdued insignias (black) on our olive drab nomex flight suits, and I noticed that the new captain had not taken care of that detail. When Captain Storm announced the party information, I asked the new captain if he was a Ranger. He said, "Yes sir, and I'm Airborne too." I said, "Great, go get all your accouterments sewn on your flight suit, and we'll go to the reunion tonight."

The reunion turned out to be a cookout with a lot of beer guzzling. After a couple of hours of beer consumption, an argument ensued between a couple of Rangers regarding who was tougher, the winter or the summer Ranger. There were no Ranger units in 1969, so the bond between Rangers was limited to experiences gained during Ranger Schooling. I happened to go through Ranger School during the summer and was thankful there wasn't any more hardship, like cold weather, added to the curriculum. From my perspective,

145

winter Rangers would be the tougher if there was a sober answer to the argument.

I wasn't involved in the discussion, but the dispute entered a whole new realm when a summer Ranger appeared at the door with a couple of what appeared to be huge june bugs, each about the size of a small sparrow. He ate them as if they were Fritos chips. Not to be outdone, others began grabbing these flying Fritos and eating them. I started gulping beer, for I knew what was soon going down. Yes, I did it! I don't think that bug hit the sides of my esophagus as it traveled down, together with all the beer I could guzzle with it. It's amazing what beer and bravado will make you do.

The new captain followed my lead, and I kiddingly said to him as he was about to swallow, "Aren't you glad I ask you to have that Ranger tab sewn on today!" The ironic thing about that comment is that he should not have had the Ranger tab or the Airborne wings sewn on his uniform. As this captain began to settle in, he told some pretty unsettling and unbelievable stories. I began to get suspicious, did a little investigating, and found that he had never attended Ranger or Airborne training. That story, like many other exaggerated tales, were his unfortunate way of trying to be accepted. Mark Twain once said, "When you tell the truth, you never have to worry about your lousy memory." This fellow definitely had a problem, and I was trying to decide how I was going to handle the situation. I was livid yet saddened by his behavior.

I was about ready to discuss the issue with my boss, Winged Warrior 6, when Sergeant Lee, the operations NCO, reported to me that one of our aircraft had been hit by a 122 mm rocket at Ben Hoa Airfield. The captain whose fate I was contemplating was one of the pilots on board the aircraft. The rocket impacted right next to the Chinook and it burst into flames. All five crewmen were burned, but none had life threatening injuries and most were second degree burns. Colonel Toner and I flew in his Huey to the aircraft. It wasn't hard to spot as we approached the airfield as it was still smoldering. From wheels to rotor hubs, the Chinook is nineteen feet high. When Colonel Toner and I walked to it, there was not a single part on the aircraft more than three feet high. We saw three of the crewmen in the hospital at Long Bien; the other two, including the captain, had already been evacuated. None would ever return to the unit for duty.

It was my unfortunate duty to give the captain another serious burn by way of some derogatory remarks in his efficiency report regarding noted deficiencies in honesty and integrity. I hope he fully recovered from all his burns.

The destroyed Chinook would be the fourth of five Crimson Tide aircraft that I would see destroyed during the remainder of my command tour. You will read about the final one in the following pages.

War Trophies at Any Price

During the Cambodian campaign I kept seeing pilots and crew members with all kinds of NVA weapons—rifles and pistols, but more SKS rifles than anything else. I began to wonder how they got them. True, we were carrying them out of The City and Rock Island East by the sling load, but nobody on the ground was presenting us with war trophies. At least that was my experience as I carried sling load after sling load of weapons from those two captured supply bases. Then I got the most stunning explanation imaginable.

We had people who were actually climbing down the cargo opening, past the hook, and into the sling load nets while the aircraft was airborne, then passing the weapons up through the cargo opening before clambering up the net and back into the aircraft. Holy Moly! Involuntary release of sling loads was not common, but it did happen. *My god*, I thought, *how in the world would I write some wife or mother and explain that their husband or son had been killed while trying to loot a war trophy?*

It was time for a safety meeting. I assembled all pilots and crew members and laid down the law. I was not seeking names of those misguided men who had already performed the feat. I told them if anybody deserved the Dudley Do-right award, it would be them. Then, with less levity, I told them that if it happened again, I would trade them a court marshal for their war trophy. I didn't bring home a war trophy, so I guess my safety meeting was effective.

My Longest Day

The fatal crash at Quan Loi on March 9 and the loss of the Chinook on the opening day of the Cambodian Incursion had brought us down to fourteen aircraft. We picked up a new CH-47B in early June and put it into service immediately. No other CH-47 before or since has likely beaten this bird to its first and second periodic inspection (one hundred hour inspection). The periodic gets more involved and prolonged as the aircraft ages; but early on, the periodic maintenance inspection entails not much more than what is required during the intermediate inspection that is conducted at twenty-five hour intervals. By the last week in July, we were on track to set a CH-47 flying hour record for a single month. On July 30, the aircraft had 221 hours for the month and our goal was to reach 228 hours—the numerical designation of our battalion, the 228th ASHB. I was scheduled to fly the aircraft on the thirty-first and had no doubts about achieving our goal, since we were averaging about twelve hours flying time per day on all of our aircraft.

The remarkable thing about setting a CH-47 monthly flying hour record had more to do with the endurance and performance of the flight crew than the aircraft's feat. The flight engineer, crew chief, and door gunner had been virtually living on the aircraft since it went into service. I had decided about mid-July that the entire flight crew should be rewarded for their performance and dedicated effort. I arranged for each to be awarded an Army Commendation Medal (ARCOM), to be presented as an impact award. Impact awards, or awards presented on the spot, require Assistant Division Commander approval. We not only got approval but were informed that one of the ADCs, BG Burton I believe, had indicated he would like to try to make the presentation. The 228th was indeed popular with the brass. The presentation was scheduled for 1600 hours. The flight crew didn't have a clue about the awards. We would fly most of the day, then break away from the AO in time to taxi up to the front of our maintenance hangar where the ceremony would take place.

The day started out normally enough. My co-pilot for the day was Captain Bill Norton. Bill was a fun guy to fly with and a good pilot. It was early in the morning, and we were hauling a sling load of bull-dozer tracks at an altitude of about three thousand feet. We had just departed Phuoc Vinh and were about ten miles north, heading to the Song Be area. Bill and I were looking forward to our two milestones that day, the awards ceremony and getting the 228 plus hours on the aircraft for the month. It started out to be one of those hours and hours of boredom days. We had flown most of the morning hauling ammunition, then about mid-day the boredom was interrupted with some of those moments of stark terror.

The Chinook has two hydraulic systems. The systems are interrelated, but one serves as a backup if the other fails. The Chinook also has another small utility hydraulic system to operate such things as the engine auxiliary power unit, the ramp, the hook release mechanism, and the brakes, but the two main systems are the babies that enable the pilot to control the aircraft. Both gauges are positioned right in the middle of instrument panel, one on top of the other, and each look real good when their needles are pointing to 3000 PSI. As mentioned earlier in this section, CW3 Getz experienced the only dual hydraulic failure in flight and was killed while attempting to land the aircraft. I was the first to notice the needle on the top gauge begin to fall. It dropped to about 2000 PSI fast. We had just passed over a FSB, so I called our operations, reported my position, our problem, and where we were landing. While I was transmitting, the needle continued to fall. Then Bill and I really puckered when we saw the other needle start its downward movement. I transmitted an emergency mayday call, then reduced airspeed, leveled the rotors of the aircraft, and set a slow rate of descent, about fifty feet per minute or less. I knew if we lost both systems we would be unable to maneuver the controls, so essentially the attitude and rate of descent that was I was trimming up would be the one we would be touching down with after we lost both systems. If we were lucky, we would maintain the level attitude and low rate of descent all the way down, but we had a lot of altitude to lose. The dirt road running north from the Fire Support Base ran all the way up to An Loc. It was flat, straight, and clear of trees, thanks to the Army engineers. We needed a long runway because our low rate of descent would likely take us almost to An Loc, some ten miles to our north. Bill was busy on the radio, talking to our base operations and to other aircraft responding to our mayday call. I had told him to punch off the load as I was trimming up the aircraft.

What happened next was frightening. When the needle on the top gauge dropped below 1200 PSI, the bottom gauge needle would follow its downward path toward the same 1200 PSI mark, then as it met the 1200 PSI mark, the top needle would shoot back toward 3000 PSI. This exchange went back and forth several times, and each time the systems' needle indicators met at their respective 1200 PSI marks, the aircraft sort of shuddered and yawed to the right. I was making small adjustments with the cyclic trim button and to the collective as we continued to watch the needles seesaw back and forth. The aircraft responded well to each adjustment, and I began to gain confidence that we might be able to make a safe, controllable landing under power. I did not want to want to autorotate because I was still afraid we might lose everything and the rate of descent would then be too great for survival. I finally decided to make a slow turn back to the Fire Support Base and increased my rate of descent. As we approached the Fire Support Base helipad, I started to begin breathing normally again, but there was not a word being spoken inside the aircraft. As I started to flare and pull a little pitch to decelerate my approach, the flight engineer said over the intercom, "Sir, your load's one hundred feet off the ground!" I yelled back in the intercom, "What frigging load?" Bill had never heard me tell him to release/punch off the bulldozer tracks, so we saved the load and landed safely.

It was comforting to see two Cobra gun ships overhead shortly after we landed safely. Less than an hour later, Captain John Smith and Mr. Glenn Miller were standing next to us, together with a maintenance team. A pin-sized hole was found in one of the hydraulic lines, it was repaired or replaced, and we were flyable again within a couple of hours. The experience was only the second time in two tours that I feared for my life, but it would not be the last time. The next would come sooner than I could imagine.

We flew sorties out of and into Fire Support Bases in and around the Fishhook and Loc Ninh area until it was time to head south to

Phouc Vinh for the awards ceremony. The monsoon season in Vietnam begins in April and lasts until October. Our flying had been hampered several days after the Cambodian Incursion with heavy rains, low ceilings, and poor visibility. The weather in the morning hours of July 31 was good for the monsoon season but began to deteriorate in the afternoon. About twenty miles north of Phuoc Vinh, I saw what appeared to be a meteorology textbook picture of a squall line. It extended all across the horizon from east to west like a huge gray trough. It appeared to be moving north. I presumed it had just passed over Phouc Vinh. I had encountered similar squall lines in Vietnam and usually punched through them in a matter of seconds.

When we had first broke off from our mission work, I had noticed that the weather looked much worse in the direction of our destination, so I called Paris Control out of Saigon and requested a radar vector for our flight back to Phouc Vinh. While we were en route, I tried contacting Paris Control again to check the weather but could not raise them. As we got closer to the squall line I could tell that there was a lot of associated rain. When we were about to enter its cloudbank, we passed directly over the same FSB where we made our forced landing earlier in the day. I had thought about landing there again and letting the squall line pass, but we were getting close to that 1600-hour ceremony time, and I did not want to keep a brigadier general waiting.

We entered the squall line and there was indeed lots of rain and plenty of turbulence too. We flew long enough to discourage my thinking that we could rapidly punch through it. I did a 180 degree turn with a new and more sensible plan that would fly us back to that Fire Support Base we had just flown over, land there, and wait out the weather. I was able to contact my base operations and apprise them of our intentions so that they, in turn, could tell the general of our delay. The squall line was moving fast, because when we broke out of it to the north, it had already passed the Fire Support Base. We overflew it, turned back to find it, but couldn't. In our frustration at not being able to find it, we were flying on the leading edge of the fast moving squall line. We were totally VFR, with our eyes out the cockpit, trying to find that Fire Support Base. We spent about ten minutes looking, then I decided that we would fly westward and attempt to fly around the squall line.

152

About ten minutes later, one of us noticed that there were no bomb craters below us. This could mean only one thing. We had to be flying in Cambodian air space, because you couldn't find a square mile in the III Corps area without bomb craters. By now Bill and I started to realize that our problem was a little more serious than missing an award ceremony and keeping a general waiting. We were running low on fuel and realized that we had no idea where we were at the moment. Then I saw it. It was LZ East, the LZ in Cambodia where Harry Stevens had clipped some trees, damaged his rotors, became unflyable, and had to remain over night with his aircraft until a recovery could be attempted the following morning. I was familiar with the LZ because I had orbited above it in a Huey long enough to watch Crimson Tide 6619114 fall from about five hundred feet during the recovery operation. Lord knows what would have happened if I had not been familiar with that abandoned LZ.

I looked at my map and determined that the closest fuel to LZ East was a Special Forces site named Katum. It was located on the southwest border of Parrot's Beak, due north of Tay Ninh. It was a good forty nautical miles away on a westerly heading. I drew a line from LZ East to Katum on my 1:50,000 map, determined the azimuth, then set course for our quest for fuel. The ceiling and visibility deteriorated, and we dropped the aircraft down just above the trees. I maintained my heading without a degree of deviation. When the fuel warning light came on, indicating that we had twenty minutes of remaining fuel, it was deja vu all over again. I was experiencing the same feeling I had just a few hours earlier while looking at hydraulic gauges. When the light came on we were going through a torrential rainstorm, reducing our visibility to about quarter of a mile. The bright yellow of the of the fuel warning light was disconcerting enough, but the jungle below was on our minds.

I was sure that we were going to run out of fuel and that I would soon be flaring the aircraft out to kill off the forward airspeed then falling downward through the triple canopy jungle below. I also knew, by time and distance, that we had to be close to Katum. I had flown into Katum several times during the last tour and was familiar with the road that ran from Tay Ninh, northbound, past Nui Ba Den (the mountain), and into the Special Forces base, Katum. I also knew that we were in the vicinity of the many NVA infiltration routes from

153

Cambodia to South Vietnam. There was not a more dangerous place to be in Vietnam if one was forced to escape and evade. I told the crew to strap themselves in because I thought we would probably be going down soon. I had no sooner said that when we broke out into clearing of about one mile in diameter. It was Katum. If I see heaven, it couldn't be as beautiful as those gun emplacements, bunkers, and vehicles looked to me as we flew directly over them. We had hit that damn Katum right on the button after flying some forty miles of dead reckoning, mostly over jungle terrain, and in some of the worst weather I have ever flown in before or since.

Fully fueled, a B model Chinook takes a little over one thousand gallons of JP4. We completely emptied two five hundred gallon rubber blivets at Katum. The squall line had passed to the north and we had an uneventful thirty minute flight back to Phuoc Vinh. The crewman received their Army Commendation Medals, sans the general. He was not able to make it because of a more pressing priority. When the green weenies were being pinned on the flight suits of our crewmen by Winged Warrior 6, I was thinking that these guys sure deserved one hell of a lot more.

It was about 1800 hours, and we still had five birds out. The sorties remaining did not warrant our return to the AO. Bill and I felt pretty good—and pretty lucky too. We had accomplished both our objectives, albeit we had also, in the process, accelerated our aging process. Our well deserving crewmen had been presented their due awards and we had achieved a new monthly flying record for a Chinook. We had our 228 hours. Whoopee!

The sorties went on and on that evening, much longer than we had been led to believe. I was in our operations, monitoring the radio calls of our aircraft and waiting for their release. About 2100 hours we got a call from one of our pilots, who reported that he was having trouble finding Song Be, his destination. Song Be's ADF radio signal was inoperative, and he was having a problem in finding the base. It can get real black when there are no moon and stars in that area, and it was definitely overcast. He also reported that he was running low on fuel. Twenty minutes later he announced that he was shutting down one engine to conserve fuel. He was communicating with several of our aircraft working in the AO, but nobody had visual contact with him. Crimson Tide 6718485 was about to run out of fuel in the

154

AO. I sympathized with the aircraft commander. I had been in his shoes just a few hours earlier. About the time 485 ran out of fuel, one of our aircraft spotted his grimes light as he was descending. *Crimson Tide* 485 had found what we would call a tight confined area and had made a beautiful autorotative landing with minimum damage.

The aircraft who spotted 485 going down orbited above the downed aircraft and reported that it appeared to have blade damage while coming down through the trees. We thankfully learned that there were 1st Air Cavalry Infantry units nearby and that the area was considered relatively safe. When we had gunships in the area, we asked our orbiting aircraft if he could find a landing area nearby to rescue the 485 crew. The 485 crew took out the secure radio and everything else they could carry and climbed aboard their rescue bird. The aircraft was secured for the evening with the infantry in the vicinity. We planned and prepared for the recovery of 485 the next day. When the pilots returned to Phouc Vinh, we learned that we would need engineer support because some nearby trees, narrowly missed during the autorotation, could obstruct a recovery by another aircraft or even a fly away by 485 if that was possible. I wanted a fly away, because I was not confident with having another one of our aircraft carried by a CH-47C model, but the "Super C" recovery team was notified for a possible mission.

July 31, 1970, was about to become history for me. The twenty-four hours of July 31, 1970, would be my longest day of my life. Thirty-plus years later, I still haven't experienced another like it. When I pulled my pancho liner over me that night, I realized that I was both physically and mentally exhausted. But I fell asleep knowing that we had not lost anybody that day, including me, and it appeared that we still had thirteen flyable aircraft.

The postscript to this story is not good. The following day, August 1, 1970, we flew a maintenance team and engineers to help recover the aircraft. It was quickly determined that the aircraft would have to be recovered by the "Super C," and the engineers went to work clearing trees. Using det cord one huge tree fell squarely across the aft pylon, extensively damaging both engines. The maintenance team took everything salvageable off the aircraft, and the engineers painted a big red X on its topside. Crimson Tide 6718485 would become a target for the U.S. Air Force sortie and would be the last of five CH-47B aircraft destroyed on my watch. Despite replacement aircraft, our fleet of sixteen Chinooks was at times down to thirteen. Amazingly our maintenance team was able to keep our required six aircraft in the AO seven days a week .

Above the Best

A Tactical Emergency or "Tac E" is an unscheduled mission that takes priority over all aerial missions. In the First Air Cavalry Division, a Tac E would only be made if the declarer was under attack and resupply was necessary to repress the attacker. We received an inordinate number of Tac E missions during the Cambodian campaign. The favorite time for a NVA attack was just before midnight. The attack typically began with a rocket and/or mortar barrage, followed by an infantry or sapper assault on the fire base perimeter. Our operations generally got the Tac E sometime between midnight to one o'clock in the morning, and we always scheduled standby pilots to eliminate confusion in the middle of the night.

Around midnight on June 24, 1970, our operations received a call from the Division TOC stating that a Tac E had been declared at Fire Base Bronco. Beehive artillery rounds, already rigged in a sling load, were being carried to our flight line to expedite delivery. Subsequent sorties if required, would be picked up and delivered from Song Be. The designated aircraft commander for this mission was CWO Larry Covey. Larry was a WO1 but well experienced. He, along with other W1s, namely Steve Lindholm and John Dearing, was considered among the best aircraft commanders in our company. The weather that night was abysmal. It was, in fact, zero-zero weather—as in a ceiling down to the deck and zilch for visibility. I watched CWO Covey during his briefing in operations, and he appeared as calm as if he were being missioned for a routine ash and trash milk run. We talked about use of the transponder and getting a radar vector, but finding FSB Bronco was going to be the challenge. If the weather there was as bad as it was at Phuoc Vinh, then it would be difficult at best.

The transmission of the Tac E did use words like "breaching the perimeter" and "expending last available," so this was a true Tac E and our effort could save lives. Our takeoff was, in fact, delayed because the truck delivering the sling load of ammunition got sidetracked and missed a turn because of the poor visibility. I went with the flight crew to the flight line and waited for the delivery of the ammo. The ammo was off-loaded right in front of the revetment so that CWO Covey could just taxi forward, lift to a hover, hook up, and go. I will never forget that takeoff. The grimes light disappeared in the overcast and fog almost immediately.

Our Tac E sortie was underway, and it would be about a thirty minute flight to FSB Bronco. We monitored his flight northbound from our radios in operations. CWO Covey had gotten a radar vector from Saigon's ATC, Paris Control. That would get him in the grid square. Getting down to *terra firma* would be the problem. The terrain around Bronco was not flat like most of III Corps. There were plateaus and hills, and that would present a problem when an approach, most likely under IFR conditions, was attempted into the fire base. Then too, besides the weather, if Bronco was under attack, he could expect enemy fire upon his approach.

He arrived in the vicinity of Bronco but was still flying totally on instruments with no visual contact with anything but the instruments in his cockpit. We could not pick up the ground FM radio traffic at Bronco but could hear some of Covey's radio transmissions as he was attempting to find the firebase. It was evident that Bronco was still under attack, and they were using flares to illuminate the perimeter. Larry could not see the flares, so resorted to using a FM homing instrument unique in the Chinook's array of navigational equipment. The vertical indicator would deviate right or left in the direction of the keyed FM mike on the ground. We knew he was using this navigational method because we heard him continually directing the ground radio operator to key his mike. We called it a poor man's ILS, but it found a lot of LZs during periods of low visibility when popped smoke was useless. It worked this night for CWO Covey. We heard him transmit that he had the flares in sight and was descending toward Bronco. We cheered in our operations for his success and his balls.

What we did not know was that he successfully delivered his load under fire and received some battle damage, although the bullet holes in the aircraft would not be detected until the aircraft returned to Phuoc Vinh. On the way to Song Be to pick up another load of artillery ammunition, CWO Covey heard a distress call from a AH-1G Cobra

158

pilot who was above the overcast, hopelessly lost, and running low on fuel. CWO Covey located the AH-G, flew to it, then led the Cobra safely to Song Be. When he returned to Bronco, the attack had been repelled, and after releasing his load, he returned to Phuoc Vinh.

What CWO Covey had accomplished was phenomenal. He had delivered needed ammunition to a fire base under attack and in the absolute worst weather imaginable. He may have saved the day for Bronco; he certainly saved the day for a Cobra pilot. For his heroism while participating in aerial flight, CW1 Lawrence Covey was awarded the Distinguished Flying Cross. Tragically Larry Covey would be killed in a civilian helicopter accident in Medford, Oregon, almost eighteen years later.

All the Right Stuff
(In the Right Place)

Sometime during my tour I flew a mission with a CW2 NFG. It was his first mission in the AO, and he appeared nervous. I thought it was because he was flying with his commanding officer, but the worst (or perhaps the best thing) that might have happened during that flight happened. We were shot at and hit! One of the rounds ricocheted off something in the cockpit and landed on the radio console between my seat and his. I picked up the bullet with my nomex/leather flight gloves and could feel the intense heat and dropped it back on the console. I looked into his eyes; they were as big as silver dollars. He was scared to death. It was evident in his reaction to the incident and noticeable in his behavior for the rest of the flight.

We talked about it during the day and I explained that getting hit happened rather infrequently, but I could tell he was shaken. I asked that he be scheduled subsequently with strong pilots like Captain Storm, Captain Mohler, and CW3 Stevens. All reported what I feared. He was convinced he was going to be killed and was terrified every minute he was airborne. All reports, however, indicated that he was very knowledgeable of the aircraft. I ask Captain Smith, the maintenance officer, to take him on a couple of test flights and to see if he might work out as a maintenance test pilot and perhaps a maintenance supervisor somewhere. It worked out. He performed superbly and made a real contribution to our company. There is never a wrong time to do the right thing. I had salvaged a pilot who made a good contribution to keeping our aircraft availability where it had to be. It was one of my better decisions during my command tour with the Crimson Tide.

Copa Cabana Closures
at Phuoe Vinh

Right at the end of my tour as commander of the Crimson Tide, the Army experienced a scandal in the club system. It involved grand larceny, committed by well-known noncoms. It shook the Army, right to the corps. When the news hit the *Stars and Stripes*, somebody with horsepower in the 1st Air Cavalry Division published and distributed a division-wide edict, ordering the immediate closure of all unit clubs. It was the classic example of overreaction and made nobody happy; not even the chaplains who, after all, were mission responsible for promoting both troop morals and morale. Club closure affected troop morale, big time! There is an old Army saying that goes, "A bitching Army is a happy Army!" This decision may have been an exception to that thesis. It was, in fact, the first time I ever heard the acronym, BOHICA, which translates to mean, "Bend over, here it comes again!"

Besides morale, closing unit clubs presented another problem. It was not as if the Cav was introducing prohibition, because the beer tap wasn't being closed. In quantity, the number of pallets of beer being delivered to the division was almost equal to the number of pallets of class V (ammo). The beer was still coming, and the beer would be consumed. But where? The hooches? Outside the hooches? Where? The edict gave no instructions or suggestions in this regard.

The Crimson Tide had three clubs, one each for the officers, noncommissioned officers, and enlisted. We had a lot of money on hand, about four grand. Our order to immediately shut down the clubs included instructions regarding the liquidation of all monetary assets. It was like, get rid of it! We got the club principals together, talked it over, and decided that we would blow it all on one big bash. Dinner and show—floor show—and the raunchier, the better.

About this time we were notified that we had been chosen by our battalion to be inspected by the USARV Inspector General (IG) team. Apparently the USARV IG team was being benevolent in the war zone, as it was giving the 228th ASHB the call as to what company it wanted inspected. Now we were almost two months into the Cambodian Campaign. We were busting our asses to keep our six pack flyable each and every day. I had aviators flying two-hundred plus hours per month. Why in the hell were we getting an IG inspection? Wasn't this war?

I had learned earlier that my battalion commander at Ft. Stewart, LTC Carter, headed a USARV IG team stationed at Long Bien. I contacted him immediately when I learned that my unit had been chosen as the company to be inspected. Unfortunately, I learned that his team was not scheduled to inspect our unit, but he informed me that he could share with me some information regarding inspection parameters and standards. I would have to visit him at Long Bien since he could not send written information. It looked like the kind of help for which I was looking and hoping. Besides, we needed about three hundred and fifty big, thick, Kobe steaks that could be procured at the Long Bien commissary. Most importantly we needed a raunchy floor show. I arranged a meeting with LTC Carter to pick up the IG poop. I brought CW3 Stevens and CW3 Spaulding with me. They would get the steaks and somehow find and contract the raunchiest floor show in Vietnam. We carried a brand new Jeep on board so that we would have transportation once we landed at Long Bien.

CW3 Spaulding had just joined our unit. He had flown B-24s in WWII. His strong maintenance background made him the obvious successor for Captain John Smith as the company maintenance officer. Spaulding and Stevens were two peas in a pod. I am reminded of a descriptor that goes: Some people make things happen, some people watch things happen, and some people don't have a clue as to what is happening! Stevens and Spaulding made things happen. Always did, always will. They were doers.

We planned to meet at the Loon Foon, a Chinese restaurant right in the middle of the Long Bien installation, after we finished with our business. Colonel Carter and I arrived at the Loon Foon and found Stevens and Spaulding waiting for us. Their crestfallen expressions revealed something bad had happened. I learned that the new Jeep, with just fifty miles on its odometer, had been stolen. My first questions was, "Did they get the steaks?" Luckily they had not yet been picked up, and the floor show had been arranged. Mission accomplished, but we had lost our ride.

We learned from the Long Bien MPs that about three vehicles a day were stolen at Long Bien. The Black Market was certainly alive and well at Long Bien. I asked about the recovery rate and the answer was not promising, so we flew back to Phuoc Vinh, sans Jeep. I walked over to inform my boss, Winged Warrior 6, about the lost Jeep. Colonel Toner's response when he heard my tale of woe was, "Bob, we are in deep shit now!" It was the only swear word that I ever heard him use. I went with him to tell his boss, the 11th Group commander, Colonel Mertel. Colonel Mertel's reaction was surprisingly calm. He just said, "Well, you'd better get a survey officer on it as soon as possible," and we went on to another subject.

We never recovered the Jeep. We did have our party and our raunchy floor show, which hardly bordered on a rating of R, not the X rating that everyone wanted. Within a week or so, my time as Tide 6 was completed. I believe the dumb decision to close all unit clubs was reversed within a month or so after I moved on to my new job in the 11th Group headquarters.

Arrivederci Y'all

The change of command when I passed the guidon to the new commander was just as under-whelming as the event had been when my predecessor passed me the guidon some eight months earlier. As I look back on my reign as Crimson Tide 6, I would have to say it was the most exciting and professionally gratifying time of my life. I could go on and use a lot of superlatives to try to describe it. Suffice it to say that it was a great unit, one that came together simply because of the outstanding people in it. Our mission was to provide aerial support to sustain ground operations. We never let anybody down. The Crimson Tide in Tuscaloosa didn't win a National Championship in 1969 or 1970, but we had a National Championship team in Phuoc Vinh those two years. Guys like Covey, Dearing, Lindholm, Mohler, Norton, Stevens, and Storm were the backbone of our flying effort, but they were backed up by hundreds of guys that helped us achieve what we were missioned to do. They, the entire company of officers and men, made me look good because they were great.

New Job for Short-timer

It was quite an honor to be selected as the Group S-3, operations officer. It was a lieutenant colonel's slot, and I was a junior major. The 11th Group had two Assault Helicopter Battalions, the 227th and 229th, one assault support helicopter battalion, the 228th, a General Support Aviation Company, and the Headquarters and Headquarters Company, 11th Aviation Group. Total aircraft assets in the 11th Group was 426 helicopters. I joined the Group staff on June 22, just a week before our withdrawal from Cambodia. I had a couple of weeks with my predecessor, Major Ted Gray, who had been the S-3 throughout the planning and execution phases of the Cambodian Incursion. Essentially, he was in charge through the withdrawal phase and then would DEROS. The Group commander was Colonel Kenneth D. Mertel who had commanded the 1st Battalion, 8th Cavalry of the 1st Air Cavalry Division during its training at Ft. Benning, Georgia, deployment to South Vietnam, and combat employment in the Central Highlands during 1965-1967. He wrote *The Year of the Horse*, an excellent documentary of his unit's experiences during that period. I didn't spend a great deal of time with Colonel Mertel as his tour was coming to a close with my arrival on his staff. Colonel Mertel was first and foremost a ground soldier who was one of the pioneers of integrating aviation and infantry and calling it airmobility.

I think it was the day after Ted's departure when we got a Tac E from division. The mission was to assemble a force large enough to conduct an extraction operation at Phnom Penh Airport in Cambodia in the event that the vice president's visit there turned sour. We were given a staging site near Tay Ninh and were told to await further instructions. The force I assembled consisted of slicks, gunships, and Chinooks. Fortunately the visit went well, Air Force 2 departed Phnom Penh without incident, and we returned to Phuoc Vinh after spending most of the day at a staging field twiddling our fingers.

During my two-week transition period with Ted, I had learned that most of the planning and execution of operations was decentralized down to battalion level. Then too, we did not conduct a major operation during my couple of months as the Group S-3. Obviously, our Cambodian Incursion had given the NVA a real setback. There was sort of a lull in operations during the remainder of my tour. That doesn't mean that there was an in-country R&R by any means. We had aerial assaults, Tac Es, and some expansion of the AO eastward, but no major battles during the period July and August of 1970.

Colonel Mertel's replacement and my new boss would be Colonel James F. Hamlet. Colonel Hamlet had just graduated from the Army War College and was on his second tour to Vietnam. He had served the previous tour as the battalion commander of the 227th Assault Battalion. Veterans of a combat zone are authorized to wear their division patches on their right shoulder sleeve, so Colonel Hamlet wore the 1st Cav insignia on his right shoulder sleeve and another 1st Cav insignia on his left shoulder, since it was his current unit. He was known as a "Cav Sandwich." In fact Winged Warrior 6, LTC Toner, was one of Colonel Hamlet's company commanders when he commanded the 227th Assault Battalion, so he too was a Cav sandwich. There were a lot of Cav Sandwiches in the division. Most of the leadership were now in their second tours. We had a regular delicatessen in division headquarters.

Colonel Hamlet was great to work with. He was from the old school who believed that his place as the commander, and my place as his operations officer was where the action was and where the support was being rendered. We lived together in his command and control UH-1H. Colonel Hamlet brought something else to the division that perhaps nobody else could be more well qualified and suited to do. There was some racial strife, primarily limited to the rear echelon areas and specifically in and around the enlisted and NCO clubs. I remember the day that Colonel Hamlet rounded up some of the trouble makers. He closed the doors to his meeting, and that was the last time there was any trouble, at least during the remainder of my tour. Another incident that I remember related to a brigade commander who had run afoul of the division commander. Colonel Hamlet wanted to give the brigade commander all the help we could in order to help him overcome the problem he was having with the CG. He could have written a book on compassion and teamwork.

Col. Jim Hamlet, 11th Aviation Group, Commanding.

A few years later, 1976 I believe, Jim Hamlet and I worked in the same AO again. I was an action officer in the Office of the Deputy Chief of Staff for Personnel in the Pentagon. Major General Hamlet had his own office on E-ring of the Pentagon and was serving as Deputy Inspector General, Department of the Army. He retired in 1981 after thirty one years of active duty. General Hamlet passed away on January 5, 2001. He was a great soldier. He may fade away but certainly not in my memory or the memories of many others who worked for him and with him.

My third and final short tour of my Army career came to an end August 23, 1970. I would be one of some 40,000 Army helicopter pilots who went to Vietnam on a short tour to fly sorties in support of the best Army in the world. About 6 percent of those 40,000 were killed in Vietnam. A little more than 2,700 non-pilot crew members also have their names inscribed on the Vietnam Memorial. Of the 109 CH-47B helicopters delivered to the Army, 20 would be destroyed in Vietnam. Five of those 20 would be Crimson Tide aircraft lost during the period January - July 1970.

I have told the preceding stories in all three tours over and over through the years. Lately, there's been a lot of collaboration with old comrades for my own self-assurance that I have not exaggerated some true stories into tall tales. I have been assured that I have not. I remember someone saying that the worst thing about getting old is being lucid enough that you can remember when you were young. Writing these stories down and talking to old buddies has sure made me feel young again.

A Prayer for the
Winged Warriors of the Future

While reflecting on my past, I couldn't help thinking about my winged warrior brothers of the future. They will, undoubtedly, write about their experiences in other wars and conflicts, some that we are familiar with and others, as you read this, have yet to be fought. Unfortunately, the wisdom of Plato's words of more than two thousand years ago, "Only the dead have seen the end of war," continue to live on and on. And so, to those future winged warriors who will be going into harms way, I end this book with this short prayer: *May God bless you with brothers as brave, strong, and professional as those that I was privileged to follow, lead, and fight with during my greatest adventure.*